Twin Turbulence:

What happened when twins happened.

By: Kristin Myers

Forward

Craig...My patient husband. Thank you for listening to the rants before I figured out I could write. And for dreaming big for me, even before I was ready to dream big for myself. I love you.

Gabriel...My baby boy. You are patient. You are kind. You are loved. Thank you for providing sunshine amid stormy waters.

Taylor...My smiley T-bell. You embrace life with a contagious enthusiasm. Thank you for your commitment to sparkle.

Sydney...My sweet baby bear. Your compassion for the world around you is inspiring. Thank you for your tender love.

Mom...You continue to give me the most valuable gifts of all: your time and unconditional love. Whenever I need you, however I need you...you are always there. Thank you for helping me edit my story as I'm living it and through this time spent reflecting upon it. Most of all, thank you for demonstrating what it means to be a warrior of a mother for my children.

Dr. Sheryl Cunningham...My friend. Your editing feedback was invaluable. Thank you for the donation of your time and that literary brain of yours.

To the educators and influencers in our kids lives...Thank you for picking up where we leave off. For the love, compassion and dedication you show by doing so much more than showing up each day. For embracing our children, and encouraging them to speak loudly and proudly. We could not have found better. And to Emmy & Lizzie – you are so appreciated.

For every person that "Liked", commented, emailed, stopped me on the street: Thank you for your encouraging words. Each one of you propelled me to rise above my fears and move forward with the public nature of this project. You showered me with bold compliments instead of ignoring the elephant in the room. I will forever be thankful for your supportive friendship.

Cass Comerford...Thank you for making this book a reality. You are a marketing powerhouse. Not only did you get me to cross the finish line in a timely manner, but you made it a fun adventure along the way...neither of which I dreamt possible.

Alia Gervasi...Thank you for editing with compassion for the integrity of my story. I needed to keep it real. You helped me succeed, and made it even better.

To my kids:

Because one day you'll be all growed up.

I love you more.

Momma

Just Saying...

Eight years ago I started journaling. At first it was a means of documenting the parenting moments that I didn't want to forget. I was afraid the stories worth telling would be lost in translation if I didn't record the details. Life was coming at me faster than I could process, let alone remember. Fortunately, I discovered that writing served another very important purpose. Journaling became my most efficient coping mechanism. It was how I maintained my sanity.

When our only son Gabriel was four and our identical twin daughters, Taylor and Sydney, were both very terribly two, our home was toddler pandemonium. I was a full-time stay-at-home-mother who was simply outnumbered by my offspring. And trust me: our ornery and adventurous twins were aware of this fact! They took full advantage of my ever-distracted nature. As toddlers, they defined the cliché "Double Trouble" and wore the stamp with delightful pride.

While trying to keep up with all three kids' seemingly endless cries for attention, my patience was stretched beyond capacity on a daily basis: hour-by-hour, minute-by-minute, and second-by-second. It seemed as though I could never catch a break; our house was a swirling cluster of confused emotions. At any given moment at least one child, and *always* one twin, was whiny, hurt, sad, crabby, hungry, wet, tired, naughty, messy, or angry; therefore, disrupting and negating the other kid(s) who were otherwise peacefully pleasant.

Whenever the constant drama felt like more than I could handle, I abandoned everyone. I handed the kids off to my husband, Craig, and retreated to our bedroom. I crawled into bed and put on the Bose sound-blocking headphones that he had bought for me for my 27th birthday, per my request. I didn't ask for jewelry or clothes! With a toddler and two babies in tow I went nowhere that required more than yoga pants and a ponytail. What I coveted more than anything was peace and quiet; the gift of temporary silence was priceless. After I savored the first moment of silent stillness the headphones offered me, I opened my laptop and threw my feelings onto the computer screen.

This was my most satisfying and productive emotional release, aside from the mind-numbing glasses of red wine that I comforted myself with at night after all three kids were finally in bed, and God-willing, asleep. I had already learned the hard way that I could not use Craig as my verbal punching bag without running the risk of sacrificing our marriage. I also knew it would be frowned upon to drink my way through the early days of parenthood, so I felt very fortunate when I discovered that my keyboard provided a venue for me to rage my side of the story. My computer was the ideal listener. Never once did it interrupt me during one of my irrational rants, and it never judged my erratic and unstable emotions. My inner explosions on the computer lessened the frequency of my outer explosions, which had the tendency to be directed at my unsuspecting family.

Once my misery was justified, I would edit what I had just written in an effort to make sense of my feelings. The editing process provided me with the invaluable perspective necessary to reflect on the thoughts I had just vomited onto the screen. This period of rational reflection proved to be the most therapeutic. While I wrote from the inside out, I was able to read from the out-side-looking-in. All of a sudden I was able to laugh at the undeniable humor presented by the twins in situations which only minutes before seemed maddening. The change in perspective also forced me to be flexible and innovative in my approach to parenting for the times when I'd stumble upon a persistent problem that didn't seem to be going away in my writing. My words were proof and awareness that my own behavior and decisions were affecting our entire family. Writing things down helped me empathize with all of the characters in my family's "stories." Thankfully, writing allowed me to learn from the past in order to avoid repeating the same mistakes in the future.

Eventually, without realizing it, I started to write less and less. This was because I didn't require as much mental decompression as the kids got older and easier to manage. The girls were growing and maturing, and Craig and I had managed to iron out all of the major disciplinary wrinkles. As parents, we shared the same philosophy that no one had adequately warned us how stressful it is on a marriage to parent young children. We had no problem saying to the world "parenting is hard." We often wondered if our job was harder because of the twins, or if other parents were just not as comfortable saying it aloud?

As a result, it became my mission to turn my journal entries into a book. I wanted my children to be able to read and find comfort in what I have written when they are in the throes of raising their own families. Fortunately, they won't remember the years of their childhood when their mom felt like every day was a battle; its a good thing too, because otherwise they may opt to never have children. Instead, they will only remember the years when they were away at school all day and I actually had the time to take a shower, tidy up the house, get the laundry done, and prepare dinner. Someday when they become blissful newlyweds, these latter memories will fool them, as they did me. They too will fall victim to the fantasy.

They'll envision a day at the beach with the family much like I did. They'll believe it's possible to lounge peacefully alongside the architecturally perfect sand castle that they've all just worked together to build. Mom and Dad will hold hands and exchange loving smiles as they watch their precious children frolic through the water. They'll assume that Dad will offer Mom a parting kiss as he gets up to toss the Frisbee to the freshly groomed and obedient family dog. When the kids run to join him, he'll pick them up one by one and swirl them high in the air in glee filled circles. Someone's music will be playing nearby, offering tender background to complete the image of a perfect day.

No, they won't remember the reality. Far-gone from their memories will be the years Mom and Dad fought over whose turn it was to apply the sunscreen on the kids; who inevitably would get some in their eyes and spend the next thirty minutes screaming on Mom's lap while not cooperating to let her get it out. They won't remember how the lifejackets that kept them safe would cause their armpits to chafe. They won't remember when a frustrated sibling stomped on the sandcastle that took them hours to build. They won't remember the time someone got drilled in the head by the Frisbee that no one had figured out how to throw or catch. They won't remember when their mangy, neglected dog, sneaking into the car that day, shook sand in their eyes while drying off. They won't remember the sunburned arm that occurred because Dad accidentally

9

forgot to apply the sunscreen there. They surely won't remember the end of the day when Mom looked at Dad and said, "This is pointless. Let's get the hell out of here."

In reality, they won't remember that parenting young children is a chore. It is a labor of love. It is a process that requires an ungodly amount of grunt work, patience and constant follow-through. It isn't necessarily fun, and it is certainly not glamorous; but if approached with humility, an open-mind, a sense of humor, and realistic expectations, there are moments when it is the most rewarding job in the world. Those moments made all the hard work worthwhile.

This is not meant to be a handbook. This is just our story. These are our reactions to the constant, unexpected nature of life that was magnified because we had twins. These are our trials and errors, our ups and downs, and our in-betweens. This is our honest truth of living through the rough parts as we searched for any and all silver linings.

Chapter 1: The Before Picture

I've always had a plan. Not one of those plans in which all the specific details were mapped out, because let's face it, I'm horrible with details. I did, however, have a general "This is how I want my life to turn out" kind of a plan.

For my plan to become a reality, it didn't matter that I graduated as valedictorian of my high school class. It wasn't necessary to earn my full-ride gymnastics scholarship to Michigan State University. It wasn't important that I graduated with honors from MSU with a degree in Elementary Education.

The reason none of these accolades initially mattered is because my plan didn't require a resume. The job I dreamed of ever since I was a little girl didn't even require an interview. However, as it turned out, my aforementioned accomplishments instilled in me a strong work ethic, and a will to succeed even when the odds are stacked against me. I cultivated extreme perseverance, self-confidence, and poise; characteristics that have proven to be invaluable during the moments when my dream felt more like a nightmare.

You see, my plan was simple; I was going to marry a nice man and be a Mom. Yep...that's right. That's all I ever wanted to do for a living. Why? Because it sounded like fun and I was sure I would be really good at it.

When I met Craig at the keg of a Spartan soccer party, my years spent dedicated to the sport of gymnastics finally paid off. As fate would have it, he was the nice guy that I married. Without having a shared interest in athletics our paths may never have crossed. Thanks to gymnastics, I met my favorite soccer player.

We got married immediately following graduation. He was a financial advisor and I taught fourth grade. Teaching seemed like the profession that would best prepare me for motherhood. Two short years later, I achieved my dream. At the age of twenty-four, I became a Mom. It was fun, and all the immediate indications seemed to prove my theory; I was really good at it.

Our son, Gabriel, made parenting a joy. He was such a good baby. He slept when we wanted him to sleep. He cuddled when we were in the mood to cuddle. He only fussed when his diaper was dirty, when he was hungry, or when his feet were hot. He smiled and cooed constantly. He reached all of his developmental milestones, aside from speech, ahead of time. While he wasn't the earliest or the clearest talker, there was steady progression towards fluency and never any real cause for concern. He was perfectly capable of understanding the world around him and communicating his needs. He walked at ten months and his coordination was impeccable. Simply put, Gabe was user friendly and all systems go.

Even as he got older, he was easy. He was always cheerful. He was attentive. He was interactive and engaging. He followed the rules. He obeyed us. He was polite and kind. He was patient and always eager to please. When he was old enough to ask to play video games (aware of the fact that this was an activity that I wasn't crazy about) he would finish his request with, "If you say no, Mommy, then I will just listen." In fact, following the many times that I did say no, he listened without the slightest bit of argument. He was everyday proof as to how good I was at this job.

As another example, before we raced his matchbox cars, I would talk to him about the possible outcomes of the race to avoid the tears and the tantrums that typically accompany the disappointment of a little boy's loss of a contest.

"If my car wins, Gabe, what will you do?" I would ask to test him.

"That's easy, Mommy," he'd say. "I will just handle myself."

Inevitably, every time my car happened to win he did just that. He handled himself with dignity and grace. He may have been disappointed, but it didn't stop him from trying to beat me again with a smile on his face.

I absolutely loved my job. I adored spending all of my time with him. We did everything together. We played together. We napped together. We ate together. We ran errands together. We went on lunch-dates together. I hardly ever hired a sitter for him because he was always such a joy to be around. As far as quality time went, I maxed it out with Gabriel. He was my sunshine, and I was his whole world.

When Gabe was two, I distinctly remember calling my mom and asking her why everyone thought having a two-year-old was so terrible? I assumed that maybe those parents that were complaining weren't very good parents. Surely if they just made their child follow some rules then everything would be fine; because even though I was a fun mom, I was a tough mom. Gabe knew the meaning of the word 'no', as he heard it quite often. He understood my expectations of him and never tried to test me because I was always consistent with my consequences. I gave my discipline techniques rave reviews.

I also asked my mom why so many other new parents complained about their lives changing so drastically when a baby came along? I assumed they were selfish parents who weren't willing to give up their own needs for their child. Gabe never slowed us down or confined us to the house for a minute. We took him everywhere with us. He was happy to be part of the crowd, and we were happy to have him along. Again, it must have been our superior approach to parenting that was the cause of his ever-pleasant demeanor.

It's a good thing I didn't write a book then...

Chapter 2: Best Laid Plan...

When Gabriel was almost five months old, we traveled to my Dad's to celebrate Thanksgiving. We had so much to be thankful for that year. Our beautiful son was happy and healthy, and Craig and I had easily navigated through the minor growing pains of learning how to parent. Craig's business was continuing to grow and our finances were secure. In fact, we were exceeding any expectations I'd ever had. Life was smooth and easy. Things were great.

Prior to leaving for the three hour trip on that particular Friday, Craig caught me off guard when he called me into the bathroom and asked, "Babe, I know this is gonna sound weird, but will you look at my ball?"

"*What* did you just say?" I asked, certain I had misunderstood his request.

"My right nut is killing me and I think it's swollen. Will you see if you think it is, too?" he asked as he held his genitalia on display with both hands.

We both giggled awkwardly just like young kids do at the mention of anything sexual. Then I knelt down for a closer view.

"Move your hands, would ya?" I instructed him. "I can't tell how big they are unless you let them hang!" I told him through more giggles.

As I compared his right testicle to his left, it was obvious that his right sac was, indeed, swollen. If his left testicle was the size of a golf ball, then his right testicle was the size of an egg. We both agreed there wasn't anything he could do except to keep an eye on it to make sure it didn't get any worse. He had been working out hard recently, and we both attributed the inflammation to something he'd strained from overexertion.

15

He complained about it hurting him a few times during the car ride to my Dad's, but I really didn't have a lot of sympathy for him. He was famous for working out like he was still a Big Ten athlete even though his endurance, stamina and strength had depleted with age. He was twenty-seven years old, but exercising like he was eighteen again. I had already warned him he was going to hurt himself.

After we arrived and conducted our initial hellos, my dad asked Craig to help him bring up a table from the basement in order to accommodate enough seating for the Thanksgiving feast.

Craig looked at me wide-eyed and whispered, "Babe, I don't know if I can do it. My nut really hurts!"

Without missing a beat, I turned to my dad and volunteered, "I'll help you, Dad. Craig's ball hurts."

"HUH????" Dad blurted with confused surprise.

"*Kristin!*" Craig exclaimed, embarrassed that I had just thrown him under the bus.

Still not having any sympathy, I explained to my dad, "Superman over there can't help you because he hurt himself working out."

"He hurt his balls??" Dad asked incredulously.

"Something like that, or he just doesn't feel like helping you move the table," I said sarcastically. "Come on. Let's go, Dad."

"Well I've heard a lot of excuses to get out of manual labor, but I can definitely say I've never heard that one before!" Dad laughed.

My family then took great joy in working Craig's testicles into the punch line of every joke. He pretended to be a good sport about it, but I could tell

16

that I had overstepped my bounds. Craig didn't think it was as funny as everyone else.

Saturday morning, Craig once again summoned me into the bathroom. In a very serious voice he said, "Kristin, I know you think this is a big joke, but my ball *really* hurts! I can barely sit down, and I think it's even *bigger* today."

I could tell by his demeanor that he was concerned, so I knelt down to inspect his privates once again.

"Holy crap, babe! You're right...it's *way* bigger," I agreed with him, instantly regretting my insensitivity regarding the situation. "What do you think is going on?" I asked.

"I don't know," he said. "But it hurts like hell!"

"Let's call and make an appointment first thing Monday morning," I suggested.

"Okay," he agreed emphatically.

As it turned out though, we never made it to Monday. He could barely sleep that night, and he was more than miserable the next day during the ride home because he couldn't sit without excruciating pain. After watching him hover above the passenger seat in agony for two and a half hours, we bypassed home and went straight to the Emergency Room at Detroit's Henry Ford Hospital. The doctor prescribed an antibiotic in case it was an infection, but also ordered an ultrasound just to be on the safe side. The ultrasound was scheduled for nine o'clock that Sunday evening. This fact alone should have been an indication to me...we were not invincible.

However, in our family dynamic, it was Craig who was the pessimist and the worrier. On the other hand, I was the optimist and always

17

assumed life would be kind. Craig was still in a lot of pain, and I knew I had to be supportive when he went into panic mode. I hired a sitter to come watch Gabriel so I could go to the ultrasound with him.

After being called to the examination room, the technician handed him a sheet and instructed him to take off his pants and underwear. In order to follow her disrobing instructions, he put the sheet aside and forgot about it.

"Well this is weird!" he said as he lay on the table naked from the waist down. "I feel violated!" he declared as he scrunched up his face in embarrassment. We both started giggling like teenagers. I suppose logic got the best of us. It seemed only natural that in order to perform an ultrasound on his testicle, the technician would need unrestricted access in order to know where to place the wand. Neither one of us considered that she had given him the sheet to cover himself up.

When the technician knocked on the door, we told her to come in. When she saw Craig lying on the gurney completely exposed, she spun on her heel and covered her eyes.

"WHOA!! You can cover yourself up with the sheet *if you'd like!*" she exclaimed.

"Oh shit!!" Craig gasped with embarrassment as he quickly cupped his hands over his crotch.

I couldn't help but laugh aloud. What else was there to do?

"I thought the sheet was in case I got cold!!" Craig tried to explain, sounding like a babbling idiot. "*Babe!*" He directed the blame at me. "Why didn't you tell me?!"

"I didn't know!" I defended myself through a fit of giggles. "I figured she'd have to be able to see what she was doing!"

18

Hastily, he found the sheet and covered himself. "Okay, it's safe to turn around now!"

The poor girl was mortified. Much to Craig's dismay, she promised him that had never happened before. She also assured him she would give clearer instructions to her next patient so it would never happen again! All three of us were laughing together as she started the exam. But the laughter in the room came to a sick halt the second she placed the probe on his right testicle.

That's when my life was no longer under control.

My stomach lurched as warning signals started to blare in my head. As I looked at the perfect little marble inside of Craig's right testicle, I placed my hand over my chest in order to contain the pounding of my heart.

"What is *that*?" I asked the question we were all wondering. It didn't take a radiologist to know that something black, round, and foreign had invaded Craig's testicle. The silence in the room was terrifying.

"I'm not allowed to say anything," the technician treaded carefully, "but I will tell you I am going to send this film to your doctor tonight to make sure he sees it right away. Expect a call from him in the morning."

This couldn't be good. As we walked out of the building, Craig finally spoke, "Holy shit, babe. What was that?"

"I don't know, but it was definitely something," I answered honestly.

After returning home, we laid in bed quietly in order to avoid the "What if's?" The dreadful answers that consumed our private thoughts were too scary to mention. Denial seemed the safest path to travel until we had more information. Craig's doctor called the next morning. He referred Craig to a trusted urologist and arranged an appointment for Tuesday

19

morning. Fortunately, we would only have to navigate through Monday with quiet worry. As I called to hire a sitter for Gabriel, I realized I was just as apprehensive about this next appointment as Craig. My usual optimism was absent.

Our greatest unspoken fear on Monday became a reality on Tuesday when the urologist rendered the devastating news that the mass was indeed a tumor. A biopsy was necessary to determine if the tumor was malignant. I watched Craig's eyes nearly pop out of his head in shocked fear when the doctor informed us that the only way to perform a biopsy within his testicle was to remove the entire testicle. The urologist explained with certain clarity that if testicular cancer is caught early, then it is considered a "good cancer to get" as it is very curable. However, if diagnosed at a later stage, testicular cancer is a death sentence more often than not. We understood quickly that if Craig valued his life he had no choice but to schedule the surgery for the first available appointment on Friday.

This left only three days for Craig to process the fact that he potentially had a life-threatening cancer, as well as the fact that he was going to lose one of his testicles forever. Talk about feeling blindsided. We would learn from the biopsy if Craig had cancer, and whether or not it had spread. If it had already spread, chemotherapy and/or radiation would be necessary, both of which would render him sterile for at least five to seven years, if not forever. We both agreed that we wanted more children, so the impact this bad news had on our family was shattering. In an attempt to pick up the pieces, Craig spent every one of those three days at the sperm bank storing as much healthy sperm as possible...just in case.

When Friday arrived, Craig handled the surgery with dignity and grace (with much thanks to the Happy Cocktail the pre-op nurses injected into his IV.) Unfortunately, dignity and grace did nothing to alter the outcome; not only did Craig have testicular cancer, but it was also prone to spread. The good news was that his doctor felt very confident that it had not yet spread; she believed she had gotten it all out of his body with the removal of his testicle. No chemo or radiation would be necessary, but he was required to undergo strict and frequent observations. Craig was one testicle (and a lot of ego) short, but the fact that we would be able to conceive on our own was the silver lining.

Chapter 3: The Perfect Storm

Nearly a year later, we finally felt confident enough with Craig's health to move forward with the expansion of our family. Gabriel was eighteen months old and we both wanted him to have a sibling close in age.

Getting pregnant the first time was a piece of cake. We tried one time and we were picking out names and planning the nursery the next month. However, this time around conception was proving to be more difficult. After a few months of having the pregnancy tests read negative, we started to get a little concerned. Late night pillow talk alerted me to the fact that Craig was inflicting a lot of unnecessary pressure on himself. He was worried that his lone testicle wasn't capable of producing enough sperm to conceive; even though the doctors had assured us on several occasions that this was nothing to worry about. His remaining testicle would compensate to produce an ample supply of sperm, and natural conception was still completely possible.

In an effort to show Craig that this was our problem instead of just his, I suggested we take a month off. I wanted to be supportive of his insecurities associated with the loss of his testicle. By demonstrating patience (which is not usually a strength of mine) I hoped to relieve his anxiety and prove to him I was in no hurry. Hopefully then he would feel less pressure. We both agreed there was to be no "trying" to get pregnant that month. If we were in the mood to have sex, then so be it. If not, that was okay too. After all, we had been "doing it" as if it were our job for three months prior, and a break seemed like a breath of fresh air.

We stuck to our word. We only had sex one time that month, and it was well after ovulation. I didn't even bother to waste money on a pregnancy test because I didn't think there was any possibility that we had conceived. I wasn't at all disappointed, but I was excited to start trying again. Little did I know, time was a luxury that was not going to be afforded.

At 10:00 on a Thursday morning, I got a phone call from Craig.

"Baby, I've got some bad news." His voice was serious.

"What's wrong?" I asked casually, not even considering the possibility that bad really meant terrible.

"I just got a call from my doctor. My MRI results came back. The cancer has spread and I have to start chemo on Monday."

BOOM.

Craig's blood markers were elevated, and a lymph node next to his kidney was enlarged. Not only was the cancer back; it had spread! Craig had made it to month eleven out of twelve. At twelve months, the doctors would have considered him to be free and clear of the chance of his cancer reoccurring. I couldn't believe it. We were so close to the finish line, and now we had to start the race all over again. Only this time, it felt more like a marathon.

"Are you kidding me?" I asked, even though I knew he would never joke about this.

"No, babe. I'm not." His hollow tone was vacant of emotion.

"Oh my God." I said. "Monday??" I asked, shocked that it was happening so fast.

"Yes, Monday. I'm so sorry," he apologized. He was actually worried about me!

"Don't be sorry!" I scolded him. "You certainly didn't ask for this! We just have to figure it out, that's all." I was desperate to make sense of the situation.

Looking back, I'm amazed by how systematically we continued to react when faced with life-threatening news. Life didn't pause for a second in those shocking moments. On the contrary, it seemed to shift into overdrive. There was no time to dwell on the horror of what was just presented to us. There was too much to be done in order for our family to survive. We ignored cancer, the scary, ominous beast that it was. Instead, we focused on the variables we could control.

I told Craig that we had to hang up because I needed to call Henry Ford Hospital and request a blood test in the minute chance that we might be pregnant. While I was scheduling that, he was busy making more appointments at the sperm bank with the intentions of spending every day prior to treatment ensuring that we had enough "soldiers" on reserve.

I discovered that requesting a blood test in this day and age to find out if you're pregnant is not easy. With all the over-the-counter pregnancy tests out, it is seen as a waste of time to those working in the blood lab. I knew a blood test would give me an answer sooner than an OTC test. It wasn't until I broke down in tears as I explained Craig's situation that the nurse became understanding enough to schedule the appointment immediately. By 10:30 I was having my blood drawn with very little hope the test result would be positive. I would find out the results within the next four hours. All I could do was wait.

Finally, at 12:45 the phone rang. It was a nurse from Henry Ford. After identifying herself, she said, "Mrs. Myers, I'm calling to let you know that you are pregnant, but just barely!"

I held my breath. "Just barely?? What does that mean?" I asked, terrified to let myself feel any sort of excitement until I fully understood the situation.

"It means you are pregnant, but I've never seen indicator numbers read this low. It must have just happened!" she explained.

"Oh, thank you!" I exclaimed as I let out a huge sigh of relief. Without saying goodbye, I hung up on her. Trembling with nervous excitement, I dialed Craig's number. Tears of joy filled my eyes, even though the presence of a very dark cloud was still undeniable.

"Craig Myers. May I help you, please?" he answered.

"Babe, you are never gonna believe this!" I declared with certainty.

"What?" he asked curiously.

"We're *pregnant!*" I announced.

"NO WAY!" he answered, stunned. "Oh my gosh! That's great news, babe! I can't believe it!"

Once again, our silver lining revolved around conception. Was it possible that God was giving us little beacons of light to brighten the path we had been walking? Craig still had to fight for his life, but he'd just been given yet another reason to prevail. Instead of heading into chemo with a doom and gloom attitude, we were anxious to get it over with so we could put the cancer behind us and move on with our blessed life together.

There was no denying that the reoccurrence of Craig's cancer was a major obstacle, but as former collegiate athletes, we were both used to

25

hurdling obstacles. We had learned to trust that our meticulously trained bodies would perform on command. In the event of injury, we were conditioned to push through the pain of proper rehabilitation. We were used to coming back from behind with aggressive diligence. Our mindset was that in order to win you must believe that winning is the only possible outcome.

Chapter 4: Sick and Sicker

While we were prepared for Craig to have to endure the brutal physical battle ahead, we were taken off guard by how much my body was beaten down by my early pregnancy symptoms. While I was trying my hardest to be supportive of the toll chemo was taking on Craig, I was so nauseous I could barely keep my head vertical. I was literally green for most of the first trimester. Eating made me sick to my stomach, but not eating would make me pass out. I was hypoglycemic when I was pregnant with Gabe so I knew to watch out for it this time. I had to eat some sort of protein at least every two hours in order to keep my blood sugar stable. It seemed as if all of my pregnancy symptoms were twice as severe. I attributed this to the fact that I was two years older, and not in as good of shape. I was also distracted by the stress of Craig's cancer and treatment plan. So it made sense that this pregnancy was more difficult than the last.

One day Craig walked into the kitchen to find me draped over the countertop with my head resting on the hard granite surface. I was extremely depressed and I couldn't stop the tears from falling.

"What's the matter, Kristin?" he asked, assuming there was something seriously wrong. He knew it was typically not in my nature to cry. I had been taught to "suck it up" ever since I was a young gymnast. When the rips on my hands would bleed as I swung on the bars, my required amount of repetitions still remained the same. Crying didn't fix anything; it only wasted time and prolonged the pain. I was trained to conquer my emotions with mental toughness. Because of this, Craig rarely saw me upset enough to be reduced to tears.

"I'm so tired of eating!" I cried harder. "I'm not even hungry, but I have no choice but to stuff my face! Nothing tastes good and it makes me want to throw up. I don't even know what to eat anymore!" I complained to him, sounding more than frustrated.

Even though I knew it was ridiculous, it felt good to crumble. With the serious complexity of all we were dealing with, crying over something as meaningless as food was extraordinarily comforting. I didn't even care when Craig giggled as he wrapped me in his arms to console me. His hug transformed my tears into laughter, because I knew he shared in my frustrations. I was tired of not feeling good. He was tired of not feeling good. I was tired of him not feeling good, and he was tired of me not feeling good. Unfortunately, the only way to break the cycle was to wait for the end of my first trimester and the completion of chemotherapy.

Those twelve weeks were unbearably long for all three of us. Craig described his chemotherapy as three months of the most strenuous physical workout imaginable, while having the worst case of the flu ever recorded. Although the chemo exhausted Craig, he never missed a day of work. Even though he constantly felt sick, he was determined to keep pushing himself, rather than just lie around feeling horrible. This was his personal way of fighting. He believed that if he gave into the disease, then it would overtake him. In his mind, if he stayed in control of at least one part of his life, then he would win. By going to work, he could focus on something other than cancer while continuing to provide for his family, which made him feel productive. In fact, the only person at work he confided in about his disease was his partner. To provide an excuse for his sudden baldness, they conjured up a story in which Craig had lost a sporting bet resulting in him having to shave his hair off. He couldn't face being a victim at the office. He needed to forget about his cancer for a portion of every day, and work was his escape. Whether anyone at the office bought the story was questionable, because he most definitely had the sick, hollow, yellow look of a cancer patient. Thankfully, his colleagues respected his privacy and never questioned him.

In the meantime, I was at home with Gabriel who was an active toddler full of energy. I tried my hardest to keep up with him, but it was tough. Gabe went from having very restricted television time to living in front of the TV. I didn't feel well enough to play with him like he wanted me to, and he saw cartoons as a special treat. It turned out to be a great compromise. I would intentionally save *Finding Nemo* for when Craig got home from work. It was Gabe's very favorite movie; actually the only movie he would sit through from start to finish. I knew Craig was going to be exhausted when he got home from the office, and *Nemo* afforded him the luxury of relaxing on the couch while spending time with his toddler son. We must have watched it a hundred times.

While the help of our entire family was invaluable during Craig's treatment, his sister Julie's trip in from Kansas to lend moral support to her little brother is the most memorable. Julie is truly one of a kind. She is by far the quirkiest forty-something individual I've ever met. She goes to extreme lengths to be the center of attention in the room, whether it is screaming just to catch people off guard, or chasing her giant dog through the house. There is no such thing as a quiet cup of coffee over leisurely conversation when Julie is around.

As if Julie weren't hyper enough all on her own, she and Craig both share an addiction to sugar. Every visit includes the perfect pie, cake, crème Brule, Napoleon, cookie, whipped cream, etc. Since I could care less about sweets and would much prefer salty potato chips, their fixation on all-things-dessert-oriented only heightens my irritability when she is around. However, because Craig adores his big sister, I had no choice but to weather the sugar-infested storm during her visit.

During that particular time, my need for quiet calmness simply could not compete with Julie's hyper frenzy. When I learned she was coming to lend her help for an entire week, I was overwhelmed enough to drop my head right back down on the granite counter. Once I processed the initial anxiety that accompanied this news, I realized her visit would provide me with just as much relief as it would Craig. There was no way I felt up to taking him to his treatments, and it would have been impossible for me to occupy Gabriel at the hospital that long, every day.

When the door closed behind Julie and Craig each morning, I secretly reveled in the fact that I could relax quietly in my pajamas in anticipation of naptime with Gabe. I didn't have to be involved in the constant quest for "magic milkshakes," or listen to her harass the nurses as to why the chemo facility was on the wrong floor.

"What's up with the cancer ward being on the 13th floor?" she would demand to know. "That's just sick and wrong! Don't you people know that 13 is bad luck???"

I wouldn't have to cringe each day as she bit her own index finger, and then shrieked due to the self-inflicted pain as the nurses were starting Craig's IV.

30

"What are you doing?" Craig asked the first time she did it.

"Biting my finger," she answered, stating the obvious.

"Why?" he asked, confused and slightly embarrassed by her behavior.

"So you're not the only one that hurts!" she reasoned matter-of-factly.

I wouldn't have to roll my eyes as they bit their fingers together the remaining days she was in town. While their ritual offered a welcome distraction for Craig, my irritability at the time would have left me with no room for patience during their silly dramatics in the oncology ward.

I would be sure to be asleep with Gabriel by the time they returned home at 1:00. Since that's when Craig left for the office, I simply didn't have the stamina to deal with her energy one-on-one. At night, Julie would prepare a generous dinner. After we ate, Craig, Gabe, and I would assume our regular pitiful positions on the couch as she willingly cleaned up after us. Then she had no choice but to join us in our *Nemo* ritual. This is just what we did, and we did not question our monotonous routine. In fact, we looked forward to the peaceful co-existence that watching *Meemo* (as Gabe called it) offered our family. Finally, after spending four straight silent and boring evenings with us, we heard Julie giggling from her designated spot on the loveseat.

"What are you laughing at?" I asked her.

"I'm sorry," she confessed, "but you guys are *pathetic!*" She addressed the elephant in the room. We weren't insulted and we didn't even attempt to argue with her because it was true.

Whether or not we had company in town during those twelve weeks, the reality was Craig and I were miserable. It was all we could do to work up enough energy to make it to the bathroom, and then we'd have to rest once we got back. I felt guilty because I couldn't support Craig the way I had hoped to, and he certainly could not be there for me. Instead of pulling together, we were drifting apart in a sea of unending nausea. We barely spoke to each other because neither of us felt up to it. We just stared blankly at the TV night after night.

We were so down and out that, aside from Gabe, our only source of excitement was when we tuned in to American Idol. It was the year Fantasia Barrino was crowned the winner, and we didn't miss an episode because we never felt well enough to leave the house. While we had rooted for Fantasia all season long, it still took us by surprise when her victory brought us both to tears. Looking back, I realize we were identifying with her perseverance and determination to beat the odds. From the beginning she had been the underdog, yet stood on the stage at the end as the winner. Our emotional investment brought forth a tangible desire to beat our own odds.

Finally, during the sixteenth week of pregnancy, we both started to feel better. Craig had finished all nine cycles of chemotherapy and the poisons were finally starting to leave his weak body. At the same time, I still had to eat much more frequently than I would have preferred, but at least I wasn't on the verge of vomiting all day anymore.

The next Friday was the start of the long Memorial Day holiday weekend. It was also "D-Day" for Craig. At long last, his oncologist would tell us if the chemo had worked. We had planned to spend our long weekend at Walloon Lake in northern Michigan. It was either going to be a weekend full of relaxation and celebration, or it was going to be a somber weekend full of preparation for more intensive treatment to come.

32

Fortunately, Craig's oncologist delivered the great news we had hoped to hear. All indications proved treatment had been successful; there were no traces of cancer in his blood.

Hooray!! Everything was going to be okay! We were going to get our lives back. While we knew it would take time for Craig to regain his strength and build back his immune system, we were confident we had made it through the toughest challenge that would ever be presented to us. After all, what could be more stressful than enduring chemotherapy and a tough pregnancy all at the same time?

Reality would sneak up on us again that very next Tuesday.

Chapter 5: Surprise!

At long last, the day of our ultrasound had arrived. Craig was cancer-free and growing stronger every day, and I was feeling much better since reaching eighteen weeks. Life was getting back to normal, and for the first time during this pregnancy we were able to look forward with anticipation.

Throughout the course of our two pregnancies, Craig had accompanied me to every pre-natal appointment. This day wasn't any different, except at the last second we stumbled upon a dilemma: Gabriel's babysitter wasn't feeling well, and she had to cancel on us. In order for Craig to be present at the ultrasound, we would have to take Gabe along, too. Even though the situation wasn't ideal, we all headed to the hospital together.

We decided the easiest way to have Gabe along would be for me to start the appointment alone while the sonographer took all the necessary prenatal measurements. It had been our experience that the technician never showed us the screen until she was done measuring, and it seemed considerate to let her focus on her work without the distraction of a twenty-month old in the room. When my name was called, the technician agreed she would send for Craig and Gabe when it was time to look at the screen so we could all see our new baby together. The plan was simple and fair to all involved. I still had Craig's company at the appointment, but he didn't have to entertain Gabe in the small, dark ultrasound room. Gabriel would have more freedom in the waiting room, and the tech wouldn't be overcrowded or distracted while trying to work. It seemed like the perfect solution until, once again, life happened instead of my plan.

I undressed and lay on the exam table. The nurse covered my belly with the cold, blue gel while we exchanged simple pleasantries. I offered basic information regarding my pregnancy as she flipped on the monitor and started the exam.

After only a minute, she set down the ultrasonic wand and stood up. She slowly began to back away from the machine while still analyzing the monitor.

"I'll be right back," she said in a voice that was meant to sound normal and routine, but instead sounded nervous and confused. "I need to go grab my supervisor," she said, still avoiding eye contact with me.

She departed the dark room without any further explanation or words of assurance. As she disappeared into the hallway and closed the door behind her, the hairs on the back of my neck stood straight up. Obviously, she'd seen something on the screen that made her uncomfortable. During the eons it seemed to take for her to "grab" her supervisor, I worked myself into a nervous fluster.

Finally, I couldn't stand the suspense any longer. I crept off the exam table and peeked at the screen that she had intentionally turned away from me. That's when I really started to panic.

"What the hell is *that*?" I asked myself aloud. I was stunned. The image I saw looked like an unshelled peanut, not a baby.

"Oh, God," I thought. "Something must be really wrong."

What if the baby is dead? I couldn't help but wonder the worst. After all, why else would she have just left like that? What if she didn't know how to deliver the news?

"Prepare yourself," I coached myself, trying to gather all the mental strength I could muster. "They are about to give you horrible news. You have to find a way to be strong."

Be strong? How could I be strong? I was alone in a dark room with nothing but a peanut to show for a baby. Where was Craig??? If I was about to receive horrible news I wanted my security blanket with me to hold my hand as it was delivered. Unfortunately my security blanket was busy being Daddy, which trumped my desperate need for him to be Husband.

"Why do we not have a babysitter??" I grumbled. I couldn't help but dwell on the irony. Every appointment up until now had been routine. Craig had been there to offer his support, but it had never been needed. Now I was desperate for him to be by my side, and he was in the waiting room babysitting our son. This scenario didn't exist in my original version of the ultrasound plan. I was terrified to be alone at this moment, but there was no alternative.

Finally, after the longest three minutes of my life, the tech and her supervisor entered the room. By now, I had already laid back down on the exam table. They had no idea I had peeked at the screen.

"Is everything okay?" I immediately started to interrogate them. "What is going on?" I demanded to know.

"Wellllll, Mrs. Myers..." she drew out her words. I knew she was intentionally stalling in order to give herself enough time to verify what the other technician had already concluded. "At this point, we don't know that there is anything wrong," she explained at a turtle's pace while continuing to stare at the monitor.

"But?" I interrupted her slow speech, annoyed that she wouldn't just spit out whatever it was that she already knew.

"Well, the cause for concern" she treaded carefully, "is that there appears to be two heartbeats."

"What do you mean two heartbeats?" I blurted with impatience. Her words were running together, and I couldn't get them to make sense in my head.

"Mrs. Myers, from what I can see here," as she pointed at the screen, "you are pregnant with twins."

She was so calm, so cool, so matter of fact as she delivered the news that would rock our universe. As I finally comprehended that one tiny little sentence, I was overtaken with confusion and nervous excitement. I didn't know what to say or how to react. My mind was frozen even though my emotions were running the gamut. My thoughts were swirling at mach speed and it was impossible to latch onto any one feeling longer than a split second. I felt as though someone had dropped me off in the most beautiful place imaginable, but I was naked without a suitcase and possessed zero knowledge of the language.

All of a sudden I felt calm, and oddly enough, not a hundred percent surprised. All of the little clues I had chosen to ignore were quickly starting to add up. I had been twice as sick, but I had reasoned that most women suffered more severe morning sickness with each consecutive pregnancy. Everyone who knew me had commented as to how much bigger my belly was this time, but I had rationalized that women always pop sooner during their second pregnancy. Interestingly enough, Craig's mom, Ina, had warned us all along that it was twins, but we had brushed her off due to the

38

fact that she worries about everything. Because of this, we never took her outlandish predictions seriously. We even laughed at her the day she declared, "Well, if Julia Roberts can carry twins, then so can you." It was a nice vote of confidence, but we rolled our eyes and never gave it a second thought. At the thought of Ina's accurate premonition, I started to giggle. Then, suddenly, my giggling stopped; because when I thought of Ina, I thought of Craig.

"Are you okay, sweetie?" I heard one of the techs ask.

I must have turned white at the thought of my husband. To put it simply, let's just say that had Craig married a woman who didn't desire to have children, he would have been just fine with it. Don't get me wrong; he absolutely adored Gabriel. However Craig's "father's instinct" wasn't innate. Nothing about parenting came naturally to Craig. For example, when Gabe was upset Craig would pick him up, but he kept his arms outstretched instead of cuddling Gabe. Gabe would inevitably go from upset to furious as he floated in mid-air two feet away from his father. Craig would look at his son like he was crazy when Gabriel started screaming and flailing his arms, and then would want to hand him to me.

"He doesn't want me, Kristin!" he would declare, frustrated.

"Yes, he does!" I would argue back.

"I don't know what to do!" he would admit. "He's going crazy!"

"He's not going crazy, Craig," I would tell him, annoyed by his lack of intuition. "He just wants you to hold him so that he feels safe!" I explained, shocked that an explanation was necessary.

I would show Craig how to pick up his baby son and hold him close to offer him comfort. It simply did not occur to him that Gabriel was asking to be cradled and nurtured. He just assumed the kid was nuts.

The first six months of Gabriel's life had been a daily crash-course in parenting. I was the instructor and Craig was the not-so-gifted student. Thankfully, he was a hard worker who truly loved his son. I managed to teach Craig how to nurture and he eventually got the hang of pacifying his son, even though I could see him fight his flustered nerves during Gabe's crying spells.

Because I knew this about Craig, the fact that I was about to tell him he was going to be the father of three children under the age of two was daunting. I really didn't know how he'd take it. I wasn't afraid of him rejecting us, but I was worried that the news wouldn't have quite the same euphoric effect on him as it did me. I knew I was going to have to coach him to feel excitement rather than impending doom.

"Holy shit!" I blurted in a Tourette-like manner. "How am I going to tell my husband??" I laughed nervously. "He is going to freak out!" I declared with honesty.

The techs smiled uncomfortably, not sure how to process my reaction since they didn't know anything about us.

"No, really! What am I going to say to him???" I asked as I threw my head back and laughed. "He is going to flip out!!"

They now joined me in my laughter, as they could sense more playfulness in my tone than true fear of my husband.

"I want to know how you are going to carry twins?" one of the techs asked me. "You are such a teeny little thing!" she observed.

40

She was right! I was five foot one and barely over a hundred pounds. The vision of myself at nine months pregnant was utterly ridiculous. I pictured myself waddling around like a giant Mrs. Potato-Head. As the reality of the situation started to set in, I started to feel a bit hysterical. I was both excited for and terrified of the twins in my belly. They were already growing, and life was charging forward. I was pretty sure this new adventure was going to be amazing, but I also recognized that it was going to be more challenging than anything Craig and I had ever encountered together. These babies would trump joint chemotherapy and morning sickness.

How did Craig and I always manage to find ourselves in these situations?? Friends and family have always joked about the fact that we are a very entertaining couple. We'll just be going through life as normal, when out of nowhere people say, "You guys are hilarious!" We never really understand why, but apparently it's true because we hear it again and again. We were even given the nickname "The Show" at one point by my brother and his roommate. Instead of saying they were coming over to our house, they'd say, "Hey, I'm going over to The Show for dinner, you wanna come?" So if we were a spectacle before, I could only imagine how people were going react to a five person Show!

"Will you go get my husband?" I finally worked up enough nerve to ask the tech.

"Well, we can if you want," the tech offered. "But, unfortunately, we're going to have to send you downtown for a twin ultrasound. We don't have the right equipment here, and you'll need a longer appointment because it will take twice as long to measure both babies," she explained. "All we can tell for sure today is that there are two heartbeats."

"Can I at least see the heartbeats for myself so I know they're okay?" I asked.

"Sure," she said as she turned the screen to face me. "Here is one." She pointed to a blinking light at one end of the peanut.

"Okay..." I said, waiting to see the second one before getting too excited.

"And here's the other one." She moved her finger to point at a similar blinking spot at the other end of the peanut.

"Oh my God...there really are two!!!!" I squealed with surprise. I was still forcing myself to accept our reality.

"It's hard to say for sure," the tech went on to explain while continuing to map out the image in front of me, "but it looks like they are in separate sacks, but sharing one placenta."

"That's why it looks like a peanut?" I asked, trying to put it all together.

"Yep," she laughed. "The sacs are side by side. I guess it does look like a peanut!"

Once I understood what I was looking at on the screen, I finally started to make sense of my feelings. Seeing their little heartbeats eased the overwhelming fear of the two babies who would soon consume our lives. Instead, I felt giddy with excitement. Suddenly it felt natural that I was about to be the mother of twins.

I was so thankful, too. How did I deserve to be so blessed with the miracle of twins? We had only hoped for one baby, and God was giving us two! Wow!

Immediately, my mother's instinct kicked in.

"Well, does everything look okay with both heartbeats?" I asked the tech, just to be sure. After all, they were both my babies now (even though one had been secretly hiding out in my belly, completely unbeknownst to me, for the last eighteen weeks) and I wanted a full inventory and update on the progress of both of them.

"Yeah, as far as we can tell," she answered. "Both heartbeats appear to be viable. They'll let you know more downtown at your next appointment. Until then there doesn't appear to be any reason for concern," she reassured me.

Even though it was a relief to hear this, I knew I was not going to feel comfortable until that next ultrasound was over. I had already fallen in love with both of them, and I knew I would be devastated if something were to be wrong with either one.

"Well, can I go make the appointment right now?" I asked. I was in such a hurry to get it scheduled it didn't occur to me that Craig might like to see the heartbeats.

"Yes, there's really nothing more we can do today anyway," the tech agreed.

As I got dressed, I nervously rehearsed in my mind what I was going to say to Craig when I walked back into the waiting room. I was going to try to deliver the news with a straight face, so as to catch him completely off guard. Craig and I love to kid and tease each other, and I was just provided with a loaded bazooka! I couldn't pass up this opportunity to see him shake in his shoes.

I took a deep breath and made my best attempt to nonchalantly walk into the waiting room. Because he wasn't expecting to see me any place other than the ultrasound room, he was instantly confused.

"What are you doing?" he asked, perplexed. I didn't let the fact that he was still bald-headed and weak from chemo treatments stop me from having fun at his expense.

"Sweetie, I'm sorry to waste your day like this," I said as apologetically as I could. "But we're going to have to reschedule the appointment."

"What?" he asked annoyed that he'd taken off a whole morning of work to be here. "Why can't they do it?" he demanded to know.

"It's not their fault, honey, don't get upset," I offered the most consoling voice I could find as I rubbed him on the back. "It's just that they don't have the capability to do a twin ultrasound here, so we're going to have to go downtown instead," I sweetly patronized him while trying to keep a straight face. I was dying on the inside, and I couldn't keep the corners of my mouth from twitching. His mind was swirling so fast that I don't think he even noticed the smile I could no longer hide.

"What?" he glared at me. "Shut-up," he demanded, trying to wish reality away. "Seriously, Kristin, why can't we have our appointment!" It was more of a threat than a question.

I couldn't help it. I slipped and let out a smile. I tried to wipe it off my face, but I was completely flushed with excitement.

"Honey, I told you!" I said as an excited giggle escaped. "It's not their fault. They just can't do a twin ultrasound here."

"Kristin, shut *up!*" he demanded again, not finding the situation nearly as entertaining as I was. "What is going on???"

44

"We're having twins, babe!" I blurted out, no longer able to contain my laughter.

"We are not. Stop joking around!" he begged desperately. "This isn't funny anymore!"

At that moment, I looked around and realized that we were entertaining everyone sitting in the radiology waiting room. At least ten people who were awaiting their own appointments were pleasantly surprised by the intense drama that was unfolding in front of them. It was cruel of me to make such a public spectacle of my sweet husband, but the entertainment value was priceless. I looked back at Craig and burst with laughter.

"Craig, I am not kidding! There are seriously two babies in here!" I said, as I heartily patted my belly.

Still, he was in shock.

"Kristin, who did your ultrasound?" he demanded to know. "I don't believe you, and I want to talk to the person who did your ultrasound!" His voice sounded panicked.

I looked up toward the reception area only to discover that we were providing entertainment for the entire staff as well! The supervisor who told me that I was having twins was standing behind the counter with an amused smile on her face.

With a laugh, she said, "Mr. Myers, it's true. There really are two babies. We saw two heartbeats. You are going to have twins."

Craig's mouth fell open. He half laughed and half choked. He looked at me, shook his head in disbelief and began to take a few quick paces.

45

Finally, in honest exasperation, he stopped pacing, threw his hands up in the air and declared, "This is a disaster!!"

I doubled over with laughter, not surprised in the least by his reaction. At the same time, I was well aware that the other people in the waiting room who had tuned into "The Show" may not have understood that he was indeed a loving father and husband, and may have instead mistaken him for a big jerk!

I shot him a raised-eyebrow-look and glanced in the direction of our audience. When he realized that everyone was eagerly anticipating his next comment, he began to laugh at himself. He then gave me a big hug, while still shaking his head from side to side. Suddenly, he let go. He pushed me away and looked at me with his eyes bulging in horror.

"What??" I asked him, not sure what was happening inside his head.

In the most perplexed voice I've ever heard from him, again forgetting his audience, he announced his horrific revelation: "We're gonna have to get a fuckin' minivan!"

Finally, our audience stopped trying to be polite. They were all laughing as Craig and I walked out of the waiting room together still in shock. I bet ours was a story that got told over and over again. After all, how often do you get to witness a young couple with a twenty month old baby in tow discover that they're about to have twins?

Chapter 6: Spreading the News

Once I finally convinced Craig that I was indeed housing two more of his babies inside my belly, it was time to call our families. Hopping into his convertible (no wonder he was freaking out about a minivan), we weren't about to wait until we got home to share this momentous news. So we put the cell phone on speaker and dialed away. Ordinarily, on occasions such as these, Craig lets me call my parents first. But on this day, it seemed fitting that Ina be the first to know since she had predicted we were having twins from the start of my pregnancy.

Craig inherited his pessimism from his mom. Ina looks for the potential for disaster in every situation. Because of this, she has proven on more than one occasion to possess an uncanny ability to forecast the future when ridiculous events are about to occur. For example, when Craig was a child she forbade him to play backyard football with his friends because she knew he would break his arm. Of course, Craig chose to ignore his overprotective mother and went ahead and played football. It shouldn't have been a surprise that day when he returned home with a broken arm.

As we waited for his parents to answer, Craig shook his head in amazed disgust. "I can't believe she did it again," he snarled under his breath.

"Welllll?" Ina probed instead of greeted. "What is it?!" Craig's parents knew of our ultrasound and were expecting to find out the gender of their next grandchild.

"Mom," Craig replied in a very stern and serious voice. "I need to tell you something first."

"OooKaaay..." she said hesitantly, unsure of what her son was about to say.

"The next time you have one of your *feelings* and it's something major concerning my life, I wish you would keep it to yourself!" he scolded her, his voice laced with irritation.

Accompanied by one of her famous, high-pitched, nervous giggles, she repeated herself, "OooKaaay..." She had figured out by this clue what we were about to tell her, but continued to play along.

"Mom, do you remember when you told me not to play football because I would break my arm, and I did???" Craig asked, still frustrated.

"Yeessss..." she said, still giggling.

"Well, you've done it again," Craig grumbled with annoyance. "My wife is pregnant with twins, and *it's all your fault*!"

She erupted into a fit of giggles.

"*My* fault?" she disagreed. "I don't think I had anything to *do* with it!" She reverted the blame back to her son, "I think this is all on *you*, kid!"

"Mom, *you* did this to us with your silly predictions!" he argued.

"Oh my word!!" she exclaimed with excitement. "I just knew it!" She continued to giggle. "Kristin was just too big for her little body! That's the only thing that made any sense," she concluded with her simple logic.

"Well," Craig conceded, "apparently you were right."

"What are you going to DO??" she asked, as she fell right into line with her son's state of panic.

"I don't know, Mom," he admitted honestly. "But I wish you would have thought of that *before* you did this to us!!"

48

We then proceeded to call the rest of the family. We broke the news to my mom by regretfully informing her it would be best to delay a proposed trip to Disney World since traveling with two infants would be too difficult. At the time, the idea of Disney was a fun and unsuspecting way to deliver our news. Little did we know that the eventual Disney trip would be a dramatic milestone for these babies we were yet to meet.

While I was having fun using our new complex family dynamic as the punch line to our jokes, Craig was still in a state of shock. He was eerily numb and dry with sarcastic humor – not his usual demeanor. He had yet to muster a smile and it certainly didn't help him feel any better when everyone we called had the same reaction as his mother. First would come the nervous laughter followed by the unanswerable questions:

"What are you going to do?"

"How are you going to manage?"

Everyone felt compelled to share the obvious, and not-so-encouraging declaration, "Wow! You're going to have your hands full!"

It quickly became apparent that these phone calls were not helping to ease Craig's mind. Terror was still plastered all over his face. Although I was doing my best to reassure him, my excitement was not contagious.

When we arrived home I was surprised when Craig got out of the car and sat down on a patio chair. I had assumed that, as usual, he would drop me off and head straight to work. Rather than question his behavior, I took the chair beside him and we sat together in quiet stillness as Gabriel toddled through the yard. As I watched my little boy climb on a play set that only had one swing, I experienced the daunting realization that it wouldn't be long before that same play set would be obsolete due to triple

49

the occupancy. I couldn't help but wonder if Craig was thinking the same thing, but I didn't have enough nerve to ask him. Finally, he stood up and walked over to me. He reached out and gave me a great big hug. It was the first time he'd touched me since we'd left the hospital.

As he hugged me, he said sweetly, "Honey, I need you to know I love you; and...I love those babies in your belly."

Even though I already knew this, I felt a rush of relief flow through my body. After a few seconds, he pulled away just far enough so he could look into my eyes. Then, in a serious tone accompanied by a sheepish grin he proclaimed, "And I'll see you in five years."

He then kissed me, giggled, and left for work. While I thought it was a funny - and even appropriate - departure considering all that he had just been forced to accept, I was extra happy when he pulled back into the driveway that night after work!

The next morning when the alarm went off, I sat straight up in bed with panic.

"Oh my God, Craig! We're going to have *twins*!!!" I announced, scared to death.

He put his arms around me as one of his famous ear-to-ear smiles covered his face. "I know...isn't it great???"

The rollercoaster ride had already begun.

Chapter 7: Lessons Learned

The next two weeks were dominated by the excited anticipation of the next ultrasound, which would reveal the genders of our babies. Craig and I spent a lot of time discussing and analyzing all of the possible twin outcomes. We came to the conclusion that ideally we wanted one boy and one girl. We thought this would be the easiest combination because we assumed there would be less twin rivalry than if both babies were the same gender. However, if they did turn out to be the same sex, we hoped for them to be fraternal in order to avoid the confusing identity issues that we feared would surround identical twins. Finally, if they were the same gender, we decided two boys might be easier than two girls. After all, we already had practice raising a boy. The thought of two teenage girls entering puberty at the same time caused us to shiver. Besides, I have always been a tomboy and easily tire of the girly-girl drama that often accompanies a group of females. Because of that, having a sister never appealed to me. I was always completely satisfied with my big brother. Did I want two bratty girls to contend with? No, thank you. Craig and I tend to be an open book, so we had no problems telling people our thoughts on this subject without considering we might have to eat our words.

This time, it was my mom that was the gypsy.

"Kristin, you'd better prepare yourself," she warned me over and over again. "You are going to have two girls and they are going to be identical." Then she'd squeal with excitement, "Oh, I can just see their little blonde pigtails a'swingin' now!!"

"Ugh," I would grunt and roll my eyes. "You better not be right."

"I'm gonna be!" she'd assure me. "And it's going to be so much fun!"

Every time she'd say it, all I could envision was a sea of pink - pink fingernails, pink dresses, pink hair bows and pink Barbie Dolls. I hated playing Barbie. I could contend with one girl, but the thought of two girls was overwhelming.

The following week I was once again lying on the ultrasound table, but this time Craig was by my side as the tech started to conduct the measurements.

"So does it look like we're going to be able to find out the genders today?" I asked impatiently. I was too excited to wait until the end of the appointment.

"Let me see," the technician answered, as she began scanning both babies for the appropriate clues.

"So what are you hoping for?" she asked while staring at the screen, still searching.

"We're hoping for one girl to be in there," I answered honestly.

"Well," she said with a sly smile, "would you settle for two that are identical?"

"Identical girls?" I asked, astonished that I hadn't willed this very combination away.

"Are you *sure*?" Craig asked the technician.

"Well, I'm sure they are both girls. I can only find one placenta, which leads me to believe they're identical," she explained.

"Oh my gosh!" I laughed, as I looked at Craig. "Babe, can you believe it?" I asked him.

"Babe, I'd believe anything at this point," he admitted. "We should have known they were girls," he snorted. "They've been sneaky from the start."

We both laughed. I couldn't argue with his logic. To my pleasant surprise, I wasn't the least bit disappointed. Instead, the idea of identical little girls made my heart swell and overflow with love. My mind flashed forward to a contented image of them holding hands as they walked together through tall grass. Their blonde ponytails swung from side to side as white butterflies flitted about. They giggled as they spun in their white cotton dresses adorned with soft bows. I could feel the bond they shared as sisters and hear the laughs they shared as best friends. I felt calmed and comforted by the unspoken security they offered to each other. In this vision I saw no pink. I had already redefined what it was going to mean to have two daughters.

Identical girls would be the perfect addition to our family, and Gabriel would be the proud big brother to his beautiful twin sisters. They would all share the spotlight instead of having to fight over it. I was so sure of this combination that I didn't even mind when I had to admit to my Mom that she had been right all along. God had blessed us with two daughters to complete our family. I realized that even when I thought I had all the answers, they weren't necessarily the right ones.

Over the next few months, these brief waves of serenity and the feeling that everything was going to be all right came and went without warning. For example, when I was seven months pregnant a shopping trip was necessary to equip us for the arrival of our little girls. While I had been really good about saving everything of Gabe's, it still meant we had no girl clothing and only half the gear. So with this in mind, my mom and I set out for a fun day at Babies R' Us. Imagine her surprise when halfway through the trip she found me sitting on the cold tile floor in the middle of the pack n' play aisle crying uncontrollably. We had already shopped for the additional crib, a second car seat, another highchair, a new double-stroller, and an extra supply of bottles. Our cart was full to the brim and we weren't even close to being done. I crumbled at the thought of having to buy a second pack-n-play. Since my mom was caught off guard and not sure how to respond, she sat down beside me and hugged me until I could gather my emotions enough to speak.

"What's wrong, honey??" she finally asked, not having a clue.

"Mom," I cried, "I feel like my whole house is going to be swallowed with all this baby crap! How are we ever going to have room for all of it? I feel so claustrophobic!" I admitted, even though I knew it was a ridiculous reason to have a temper tantrum. I knew I didn't have the right to complain. We were so fortunate to be able to afford to buy all that we needed to make our lives easier with twins, yet my emotions were getting the best of me. "If this is just the 'stuff' we need, how am I ever going to handle the actual *babies*?" I asked her, hoping she could offer me the encouragement I was desperate for.

"Oh, sweetie," she consoled me. "It is going to be crowded, and it *is* going to be crazy; but if anyone can do this, it's you. And we'll be there to help every step of the way!" she promised.

"I know, Mom," I said, still not satisfied. "I think the reality of having twins just now hit me. It's going to be really different this time, isn't it?" I asked, finally admitting my fear of what was to come. Still hugging on the floor of Babies R' Us, she threw back her head and laughed.

"Oh, honey," she breathed deeply. "I don't think any of us have any idea what we're in for!!" she told me honestly. "But, you know what?" she asked.

"What?" I sniffled.

"We sure are going to have some great stories to tell!" she predicted.

My mom knew exactly what I needed to hear. I was looking for my panic attack to be validated. No, I wasn't crazy for being scared. Our family was going to grow from a calm three to a hectic five in just a couple of months. Our simple life as we knew it was about to end and there wasn't going to be anything easy about it. But the laughs (and tears!) that would result while trying to figure it all out would be worth it in the long run.

As usual, my mom was right: We had no idea what we were in for.

Chapter 8: Big Anticipation

From the moment we were told we were having twins, my pregnancy took on a more complicated dynamic. I was immediately categorized as "high risk" and my doctors made it clear that I should pay very close attention to my body. Since further ultrasounds still detected only one placenta, the girls were assumed to be identical. This shared placenta only heightened the risk that more complications could arise. The babies were being monitored very closely via frequent ultrasounds, and I was given strict orders to report to the emergency room whenever something out of the ordinary occurred. By the time I reached thirty weeks, I was huge. I had gained nearly half of my body weight in less than nine months. I started my pregnancy at 105 pounds and I would deliver the girls at 155 pounds. The vast majority of that weight was centered in my belly. My premonition was correct: I did look like Mrs. Potato Head. I was 5'1" tall and almost as wide.

I began having frequent and consistent contractions. As a result, we took several false-alarm trips to the hospital, but hydration in the form of IV fluids always proved to settle the contractions down. On one occasion I actually believed that my water had broken. Six hours later the ER doctors concluded that I had simply peed my pants. My amniotic sac had not been punctured and they could find no trace of amniotic fluid in my underwear. They determined that when I sat down to rest, the weight of my enormous belly had squished my full bladder and caused me to urinate without me even knowing it. I was more than embarrassed when I realized I had wasted everyone's time because my belly was so full of babies.

One day near the end of my pregnancy, I entered the market to buy some groceries. A middle-aged man was working the checkout counter nearest the door. When he looked up and saw me, he started laughing right out loud. When he realized I had witnessed him mocking me, he covered his mouth with his hand and apologized.

"Go ahead," I said sarcastically. "Laugh all you want," I gave him permission. "I can't even argue with you."

"I'm sorry," he said embarrassed, but still unable to halt his laughter. "I've just never seen anything quite like you! You look like you should have popped a long time ago!"

"There are two in here," I condescendingly justified, holding up two fingers, "and I've still got a ways to go," I informed him.

"Well, I don't know how you're gonna make it!" he declared as I walked away to buy my groceries. I had been wondering the same thing myself. I remembered feeling like I was going to burst before I had Gabriel, who weighed 6 lb. 13 oz. Even though the girls' combined birth-weight would only be a pound more than Gabe's, I was enormous in comparison to my first pregnancy. This time I was toting around twenty-eight additional pounds, which included two babies crammed into that tiny space and two separate sacks of amniotic fluid.

All of the extra weight in my mid-region was taking a toll on my back. I was forced to wear a strong elastic harness that looked like a girdle with suspenders to help ease the load. I knew my belly was getting out of hand when I sat down in my grandma's antique caned chair and fell right through the bottom of it! I was horrified as I sat trapped in the wooden frame. My Mom and Grandma could barely stop laughing long enough to

57

help pull me out of it. All I could do was shake my head in disbelief, chuckle along with them, and let them have their fun.

To add insult to injury, there were no maternity clothes that fit me. I was too short for the large maternity sizes, but too big in the center to squeeze into the smaller ones. During the last month of my pregnancy, the only thing I could wear comfortably were Craig's XXL cotton T-shirts.

Because my lungs were so compacted from all the space the babies were occupying, even the shortest of walks left me winded. I moved like a sloth and had to sit down to rest halfway up the staircase before I could regain my breath. The week before I delivered the girls, Craig and I were at Kroger. I quickly grew irritated with him because he kept walking ahead of me. I had to beg him to slow down because I couldn't keep up with his pace.

Finally, in frustration, he turned around and snapped, "Babe! I *can't walk any slower!*" His honest admission brought tears to my eyes. Being physically limited by these two babies was exhausting. I was tired of chasing after and potty training Gabriel, who had just turned two, with an extra fifty pounds attached to me. I hated not being able to pick him up because it hurt to have his weight resting on my belly. Craig was bearing the brunt of my extra-large condition and he was tired too. All three of us were anxious for this to be done. Unfortunately, all we could do was continue to wait and pray for more patience. Our babies needed to cook as long as possible inside my belly.

Chapter 9: Rump Shaker

Near the end of my thirty-third week of pregnancy, I was once again awakened in the wee hours of the morning with frequent and painful contractions. These symptoms were much more intense than what I had experienced before, so I immediately started to drink lots of water in an effort to hydrate myself. I was hoping to slow the contractions down on my own in order to avoid wasting another trip to the ER. However, instead of slowing down, the contractions started to speed up. So at 5:00 A.M., we called friends to see if we could drop Gabriel off for the morning while we went to the emergency room. Thankfully they agreed without any hesitation.

We grabbed our overnight bag that had been packed for weeks, threw Gabriel in our new minivan, and headed to the hospital. On the way, Craig made mental a list of the calls he would have to make in order to cancel his appointments for the day. Meanwhile, Gabe and I practiced his colors by identifying the cars as they passed us. We were going through the motions, totally secure in the fact that we'd be picking him up later in the day, and life would continue just as it had before this morning.

When we arrived at the ER, the nurses followed the usual protocol of hooking me up to IV fluids, monitoring the babies' heartbeats, and leaving us to be bored out of our minds. After a little while though, the doctor came in and said he wanted to perform an ultrasound to check on the babies. I was on a bi-monthly ultrasound schedule anyway, and I was due for another one in a couple of days. He told me that if everything looked normal, I could skip my next scheduled appointment. That sounded like a great idea! At least today's visit wouldn't be a total waste of time. I was growing tired of the constant screening, and the appointments were progressively getting more uncomfortable and monotonous.

However, right from the start, this ultrasound proved to be anything but monotonous. As the technician was getting a visual on the babies, the on-call OB-GYN came in to observe. Craig and I were semi-paying attention. The tiny room was crowded, and it was hard to see the screen since they were both standing in front of it. All of a sudden, the doctor captured our full, undivided attention.

"Yep," we heard him agree with the technician. "There's one," he started to count while pointing at the screen, "two...and three."

"WHAT????????" Craig and I gasped in unison.

The doctor was startled. "You are having triplets, aren't you?" he asked, surprised we didn't already know this.

"No!" I countered with panic. "Twins!" I corrected him. "We're having *twins*!" I willed him to believe me.

I looked to Craig to offer me backup, but the blood had drained from his face. He didn't say a word, he only stared vacantly at the doctor with his mouth gaping open in terror. I grabbed his arm. I couldn't take this news alone. He had to snap back to reality because I was desperate for his reassurance and support. When my plea for help didn't faze him, I tightened my grip; not because I thought it might shake him out of his stupor, but because I was scared he might try to bolt out of the hospital never to return!

"This is not funny," I berated the doctor. "If you are joking, please *stop*! This is NOT funny!" I repeated, louder to be sure he got the point.

"Well," the doctor stammered as he turned back to reinvestigate the screen, "Let's see here..."

Finally, after analyzing the monitor for what seemed like an eternity, he pointed to a specific area on the screen.

"Can you zoom in closer right there?" he asked the technician.

As the technician manipulated the computer to bring the image closer for the doctor to see, it was now Craig who was squeezing my arm tightly. He still had not uttered a word, but I knew he was latching on to the hope that the doctor had made a mistake. So was I.

"You know what?" the doctor asked casually, while still looking at the monitor. "I think that is a rump."

"A rump?" I asked, still not understanding what he was trying to tell us.

"Yeah," he concluded, as he turned to face us, "that's a rump."

"What does that mean?" I asked, needing him to spell it out for me.

"It means you can rest easy," he said with a smile as he patted my arm. "There are only two babies in there. I mistook a rump for a third head at first glance," he explained. "Sorry about that."

Sorry about that? We could rest easy?? We both nearly had heart attacks, and he thought a pat on my arm would make it all better? I wanted to smack him.

Finally, Craig spoke.

"I think I might need a brown paper bag," he announced as he dropped his head in between his knees.

"Are you okay, honey?" I asked him, genuinely concerned.

61

"I don't know how much more of this I can take, Kristin!" he declared honestly.

"Hang in there, babe. At least there's only two, right?" I tried to console him.

"There better be two," he threatened. "Kristin, I can't do three."

"I know, babe. I know," I agreed.

Once we finally settled down from the latest scare of our lives, the doctors resumed the course of the ultrasound. Since we knew the babies were sharing a placenta, it was imperative to keep very close track of their weight differentiation. Unequal placental sharing between the babies could result in less blood flow and nutrition to one fetus, with more to the other. Put simply, if one twin absorbed too many nutrients, the other twin could starve.

Baby A had consistently measured larger in-utero than her sister, Baby B. Because the discrepancy in size had been consistent, there hadn't been any reason to worry because it fell within the normal range. Twins are rarely the same exact size and weight, and as long as the differentiation was normal there was no need for concern.

However, on this day we were informed that Baby A appeared to be one whole pound heavier than Baby B. The doctors were concerned that something in the environment of the womb had changed. It was likely Baby B was struggling to absorb the appropriate amount of nutrients, while Baby A was absorbing too many. The only reassuring part of this diagnosis was that both heartbeats were strong and healthy. So what did all this mean?

Our doctor explained to us the babies and I were going to have to be monitored constantly throughout the remainder of my pregnancy. I was admitted as an in-patient to the hospital so the doctors could subdue my contractions for as long as possible in order for the girls to continue to grow and mature. The earlier they were born, the more complications they could face. The doctors hoped to stretch my pregnancy out to thirty-six weeks for optimal development of the babies. The possibility of this prognosis would depend on further ultrasonic measurements. If they concluded there was too big of a discrepancy between the weights of the babies, I would undergo an emergency c-section to deliver them within the next forty-eight hours. The health of their lungs was critical at this stage of pregnancy so I was administered the first of two injections that would specifically amplify lung development. As a precaution, the doctors would wait to deliver the babies until after both rounds of shots had been administered, unless one of the twins went into obvious distress.

The following day I was scheduled to receive my final lung shot and undergo my third ultrasound in two days. This time, a neo-natal care specialist would be present to make the final decision as to whether or not I would have an emergency c-section. There were three collaborating doctors and a sonographer crowding the tiny screen. After taking very careful measurements, the neo-natal care specialist concurred with everyone else: Baby B was dangerously smaller than Baby A. Prior to this day, on several different occasions at several different ultrasounds I had been careful to mention that Baby B didn't seem to be as active as Baby A. While there had been no cause for concern then, this detail, in conjunction with the weight differential, landed me in the operating room just two hours

63

later.   Six weeks ahead of schedule, our tiny daughters would enter the world.

Chapter 10: Welcome to the World

When Gabriel was born, Craig wasn't allowed in the room because general anesthetic had been unexpectedly necessary for the C-section. As a result, we assumed we had missed out on one of life's most wonderful experiences. However the girls' birth would soon prove truth to the old adage "what you don't know can't hurt you."

Due to the fact this was a high-risk twin pregnancy, there were fifteen professionals in the room to assist with the delivery. In addition to my doctor, my nurse, my anesthetist and Craig, each baby had a team of three doctors and three nurses. Even though it was my belly that was being dissected, I was kept isolated from the anticipation that was abuzz in the room.

The big blue sheet that was purposefully hung to block my view of the procedure left me very frustrated. I could feel every tug and pull as the doctors prepared to separate my babies from my body. I craved detailed information, but most of my questions went unanswered. Rationally I knew the doctors and nurses were busy communicating with each other, and Craig was dutifully watching over the whole process. I tried to remain patient and calm, but I was anxious with anticipation, and my lack of knowledge morphed into suspicious fear. Why weren't they telling me any thing? What didn't they want me to know? Believe it or not, I felt left out of my own twin delivery.

Finally, at long last, my doctor informed me that they were ready to take Baby A. Occupying the left side of my belly for the last thirty-four weeks, she had made her presence known. She was forever kicking and punching me, and rumor had it she was stealing nutrients from her little sister, too. This was our feisty baby, the one who already knew how to get our attention. We couldn't wait to meet her!

I knew the second the doctor had pulled her from my belly because the room became eerily quiet. I kept waiting to hear her cry, but instead all I could hear were hushed tones and hurried conversations.

"Is everything okay?" I asked, as I could sense the tension in the air.

"It's okay, Kristin," my doctor answered calmly. "She's having some trouble breathing, but she has a very good team of doctors working to stimulate her. Right now we've got to focus on getting the second baby out safely," he cautioned me before I had a chance to worry or ask more questions.

"Okay," I said, unsure of what was going on. I chose to trust in what the doctor said and followed his orders. I was determined to be the most obedient patient I could be in order to help my babies be delivered as safely as possible. In that moment it wasn't about me. My daughters needed the full attention of their doctors, and I was not about to steal any of that from them.

I did, however, need some reassurance from my husband.

"Craig?" I summoned him nervously.

"Yeah baby?" he answered, as his head popped around to my side of the sheet.

"Is she okay?" I asked, praying for a positive answer.

"They're working on her in the other room. She's in great hands, sweetie," he promised. "You're doing great. Just keep it up," he rooted for me.

I was so frightened. If Baby A was struggling, what did that mean for my little pee-wee in there? Baby B had been so passive in comparison to her boxer of a sister. I hardly ever felt her move inside of me, and there was already cause for concern due to her low ultrasound weight.

Once again, I heard more hushed conversation and felt more tugs and pulls as the activity heightened behind the sheet.

"Is she out?" I asked, already knowing the answer as the same uncomfortable silence filled the room for the second time.

"Yes, she is," offered my doctor. "She needs a little jumpstart, too, Kristin. Her doctors are working on her and I'm going to focus on getting you closed up."

I took a deep breath and said a little prayer for my daughters. Craig came to stand by my head and leaned over to kiss me.

"You did great, honey" he praised me.

"Is Baby A breathing yet?" I asked him immediately.

"Not yet. She's having some trouble," he answered me honestly.

"Craig?" I asked him, as panic started to flood my veins.

"What, honey?" he answered as he grabbed my hand.

"I don't feel right," I said, as I was flooded with nausea. He heard the worry in my voice and could tell my coloring was off.

"Ahm, excuse me," Craig said as he tapped my anesthetist's shoulder to gain her attention.

"She doesn't look very good," he informed her. He was referring to the fact that I had turned green.

I was light-headed, my whole body felt tingly and I thought I was going to vomit. Not only was I terrified for my babies, but now I was also consumed by the fear that I was having an allergic reaction to the anesthesia.

"Okay," my anesthetist answered calmly. "She'll start feeling better soon," she reassured Craig, as she pushed another fluid into my IV.

Thankfully, my head started to clear again and the nausea started to dissipate, just as a large plastic incubator rolled up beside my head.

"Here's Baby B!" I heard a nurse announce.

"Baby B??" I automatically questioned her. "Where is Baby A?!" I demanded to know.

"She's had a tough start, but they're doing everything they can to help her," the nurse tried to reassure me. Despite the immense concern caused by this information, I was momentarily distracted from my worries by the tiniest little baby I had ever seen. She had an intubation tube taped to her mouth, and she was covered with monitors, wires, and IV tubes. Right now, none of that mattered. She was alive, and that was all I cared about. I couldn't touch her because they were taking her straight to the NICU, but I didn't mind. I would touch her later. I was more than willing to stay out of the doctors' way if that's what was best for her.

Although I was stunned by her size, she was the sweetest little thing I had ever seen. Before entering the delivery room, Craig and I were still deciding between two sets of names to call our daughters: Brianna and McKenna or Sydney and Taylor. But when I saw her, I instantly knew Brianna and McKenna were out of the running. How could something so little have a name with three syllables? Those names were too heavy for someone so small and fragile. This precious little baby needed a name that was sweet and delicate. A name that was softened at the end, like in

68

pet names such as "sweetie" or "honey." In my mind, she had named herself.

"She looks like a Sydney to me!" I pleaded to Craig.

"I completely agree," he said. "Sydney it is!" he announced happily.

"Yay!" cheered the nurses, as they rolled her away.

My heart felt full for just a brief moment. In that very same breath, I quickly learned my first twin lesson: It is impossible to think of one twin without considering the other. The euphoria of meeting Sydney quickly disappeared and was replaced by the wrenching fear for her sister's precarious state of health.

"How is she doing?" I asked nervously. By the tone of my voice, it was obvious whom I was talking about.

"Well, we had a little scare there," a masked person admitted to me. "But she's a fighter. We can tell! She's intubated and breathing now. You'll get to see her in a minute."

I was flooded with relief. I grabbed Craig's hand and squeezed.

"She's okay?" I asked him.

"She's okay, babe," he smiled back, as he exhaled an honest deep breath of relief.

I saw her incubator approaching, but, unfortunately, they couldn't pause to let me look at her as they had done with Sydney. She needed to be in the safety of the NICU immediately. Although she was covered with tubes and wires just like her sister, I could see that she was strong and beautiful. As she rolled past me, my eyes filled with tears of gratitude.

"Way to go little Taylor," I whispered to her. I was so proud of her. Craig squeezed my hand and smiled at me with tears of his own filling his

69

eyes. *All* of his girls were safe. There was still a long way to go before our sweet baby daughters would be considered healthy, but for the time being it was enough to know we had all made it out of the delivery room.

Chapter 11: The NICU

An hour later we visited our twin daughters for the first time in the Neonatal Intensive Care Unit. Instead of reveling in the joy of their birth, we were disconcerted with the uncertainty of their condition. I had been naïve to assume that making it out of the delivery room would be our largest hurdle. Their vulnerable state at birth had landed them in the Critical Care Unit of the NICU: the room in which "life or death" takes on the most literal meaning for struggling newborns. While the doctors had been successful in enabling our daughters to breathe with the aid of tubes and machines, we now had to wait to see if they would continue to develop enough strength to sustain life on their own. Our premature little babies had to fight to stay alive.

We spent a total of twelve days in the NICU. Every one of those days was clouded with an overwhelming sense of fear. Everything about the experience was scary. The room itself was cold, sterile and unwelcoming. It was full of babies in critical condition who were all confined to tiny, coffin-like, plastic incubators for at least twenty-two hours a day to safely maintain their body heat. They were covered with cords, IVs and monitors. Their eyes were bandaged shut as they baked underneath ultra-violet lights in order to rid them of jaundice. Just to gain entrance to the room, we were required to sterilize ourselves by scrubbing like surgeons from our fingertips to our elbows at the large stainless steel washbasins operated by foot pedals to minimize the spread of germs.

Once inside, it was unsettling to see infants who were treated like science experiments rather than newborn babies. Nurturing fell low on the priority list. Continued systematic development had to be the main concern. Because of this, the nursing team documented every detail that occurred during incubation. Every wet diaper was recorded, as well as every bowel movement. Bottle levels were checked and rechecked at every feeding to chart milk consumption to the nearest milliliter. The girls' vital statistics were recorded like clockwork, and they were poked daily to monitor the bilirubin in their blood. It was all business in the NICU for the nurses. Their job was to get the babies healthy enough to go home. It was the job of the parents to worry about progression towards this goal.

"Oh no. Sydney didn't finish her bottle," we would fret. Or, "Uh-oh...Taylor peed two diapers in a row, but she hasn't pooped!"

These were the hot topics of conversation.

The girls appeared to be extra fragile because they were so little. You can imagine the extreme frustration we encountered when we learned that their birth weights only differed by *one ounce*. After all the worry and concern by some of the best specialists in their field, Taylor was born weighing 3 lb. 14 oz. and Sydney followed close behind at 3 lb. 13 oz.

"Damn technology!" I cursed when I learned this fact. We couldn't help but second-guess the decision made by the doctors to deliver our daughters prematurely. If it hadn't have been for the misleading ultrasounds, the girls would have stayed in my belly longer and had more time to develop naturally.

Because they were so small, it was initially scary just to pick them up. Their tiny legs were the width of Craig's pinky finger, and he could easily cradle both girls in the palms of his hands at the same time. Their little private parts appeared to be inside out because they weren't yet fully

72

developed, and their poor little faces were all scabbed up from the tape that had held their intubation tubes in place. Taylor's lip was especially raw since she had decided to rip her tube out herself.

NICU is an acronym that strikes raw fear in the hearts of parents who have had children spend time there. No matter what the reason may be, there is no such thing as a pleasant stay in the NICU. The terror of the unknown, coupled with the shameful feeling of helplessness, nearly ripped my heart out. There was nothing I could do for my babies except to pray, trust the medical professionals, and wait for God to decide their fate.

Our stay in the NICU was complicated by the fact that we had two babies in Critical Care. When the girls were first admitted, the room was at full capacity. As a result, there was no room for Taylor and Sydney's incubators to be placed side-by-side. So every time we visited, we were forced to divide and conquer. I would sit with one baby on one side of the large room, while Craig would sit with the other baby forty feet away on the opposite side of the room. In order to visit both girls, we'd have to begrudgingly bid farewell to our first baby in order to spend time with her sister. It didn't seem fair to have to pick and choose between our daughters. As we passed each other in the middle of the room, Craig and I usually offered each other a shared eye roll and a sarcastic high-five. This was the only comic relief we could muster to combat the impersonal nature of our visits. Our daughters were treading water oceans apart. The twin bond they shared for thirty-four weeks had been thrown overboard. How would they learn to the swim the turbulent waters without the support of each other? Our feeble attempt of offering a parental life preserver here and a parental life preserver there seemed like a cruel joke.

73

In the midst of all this we still had Gabriel to consider, and it was impossible to predict how long the girls would be in the hospital. We couldn't neglect Gabe because of his baby sisters, so Craig went home in the evenings to spend time with our two-year-old. He would return to the hospital in the morning to visit the girls and me. It was hectic and confusing, but we were now the parents of three young children. We had no choice but to jump right into the balancing act that goes along with it.

Thankfully my own mother had always modeled for me an attitude of strength and optimism. Even though my mind was plagued with worry the entire time, I knew it was now my turn as Mommy to be strong for my little girls. I have to admit, the complexity of the situation made it especially challenging for me to maintain my composure.

Never having spent time in the NICU before, I was irritated due to lack of information. I wanted immediate, definitive answers to two very distinct questions: First, were they going to be okay? And, second, when could we take them home?

What I didn't realize at the time was the doctors and nurses did not have answers for these questions. What I mistook as frustrating avoidance was in fact honesty. When they told me they couldn't be sure, they were not withholding information; they simply didn't know. There was no way they could predict the future of our daughters' health. They were telling us the truth when they proclaimed that only time and observations could answer these questions.

We learned to look for our own answers by adapting the same techniques of the nursing team. Every time we changed their diaper we prayed for it to be poopy. Poop meant that their bilirubin count would decrease, thus making their jaundice go away. Every time we fed them, we worked as hard as we could to keep them awake long enough to finish their bottles. Neither one of them possessed a strong sucking mechanism, but Sydney was an especially slow eater. Even when we unwrapped her blanket and tickled her feet, we couldn't get her to stay awake long enough to drink the required amount of milk. Feeding time was nerve racking because we knew that every unfinished bottle equated to a longer stay in the NICU.

My mom, the Queen of Optimism, would practically bring her skirt and pom-poms to cheer for Sydney while she was feeding her.

"Sweetie, you have to eat so you can go home and meet your dog, Tucker!" Or, "Your big brother is waiting for his little sisters to come home so he can teach you to play choo-choo trains!" When she got really desperate, she negotiated. "Baby, Memom will buy you whatever you want if you'll just finish your bottle!"

The feeding part was especially hard for me. Although I had always assumed I would breastfeed my children, I quickly realized with Gabriel that breastfeeding was not a good fit for me. I hated every moment of it. It went beyond physical discomfort. Emotionally it threw me into a state of agitated depression, making it impossible for me to feed him with any sense of serenity or patience.

I forced myself to suffer through my discomfort for the benefit of my tiny daughters. It was the only service I could provide for them. I could only hold them for an hour three times a day since they had to stay in their warm incubators. Even then it was almost impossible to nurture them because I had to be so careful of all the cords and monitors attached to them. The

75

only thing I could do to help make them stronger was to offer them my breast milk.

Pumping for the twins was an unbelievably difficult chore. In order to supply enough milk for both of them, I had to pump every two hours, twenty-four hours a day. My body struggled to produce enough milk. It was so discouraging because I could barely fill the tiny little bottles. I couldn't help but feel like a failure.

Every bottle had to be labeled with a special color-coded sticker provided by the hospital. Every sticker had to be dated and signed in order to verify that the milk had, indeed, come from me. By the time I got all set up, pumped, labeled the bottles, and cleaned up, I only had an hour and a half before I had to start the whole process over again.

In those seemingly endless eternities when I was pumping, my mind was engulfed with a dark, sick depression. My worst fears surfaced while pumping. My optimism retreated, and I was flooded with morbid and obsessive thoughts. What would I do if one of my daughters died? Even worse, what if both of my daughters died? How could I handle that? If they did make it out of the hospital alive, how was I going to survive my new life? I was going to be consumed by all these kids. How would I maintain a sense of self without suffocating? What was going to be left of *me*? How was I ever going to find time for a shower once I was on my own with all of them? How were Craig and I going to get through this without killing each other? What if Gabriel hated me for not being able to pay as much attention to him anymore? What if I couldn't give the girls the same kind of love and attention that I gave to Gabe when he was a baby? What if I failed them all?

The dreadful questions went on and on. While I pumped tears would pour down my face. I cried almost every time. I couldn't temper the anxiety that haunted me. It was as if pumping triggered my hormones to attack my emotional stability. I would plummet into a malignant chasm of hopelessness. The only way I could regain control of my emotions was to yank the suction cups off my breasts. Once free of the pump, my confidence returned and my thoughts steadied. It was unnerving to be consumed by such morbid thoughts and narcissistic feelings.

Because breastfeeding had such an ill effect on my state of mind, it felt like an enormous sacrifice to me. I vowed to the girls that I would give them my breast milk at least until their due date, which meant that I would have to endure pumping for six full weeks. I rationalized that had they not been born prematurely, I would still be on forced bed rest in the hospital away from Gabriel, which would have been miserable, too. Breastfeeding became their reward and my self-inflicted punishment for failing to carry them to full term.

While in the NICU, I couldn't help but think of all the ways I could have prevented the situation. The inability to answer the question "Why?" was too mind-boggling to accept, so instead I assumed the guilt.

As I held my teeny-tiny babies, I chastised myself. I wished I had kept my mouth shut about Sydney's quiet nature in my womb. Maybe then the supposed weight differentiation wouldn't have seemed so alarming to the doctors. I punished myself for trusting the doctors and the ultrasounds. After all, Gabe was born weighing 6 lb. 13 oz. even though an ultrasound performed that day predicted he would be an eight-pound baby. I should have known better, damn it! Why didn't I force the doctors to wait longer before taking them? If only I had stood my ground, maybe all of this could have been avoided.

I worried about the long-term effects on the girls. Would they struggle because they were born prematurely? Had I set them up to fail? They didn't deserve to start their lives in these stupid, plastic boxes. How could they possibly be happy? They were torn from my womb, torn from each other, and thrown into isolation. Good mothers held their babies and showered them with affection. Did they even know they had a mother? Did they know that I loved them?

Even though I thought it couldn't get worse, it did. Four days later I was discharged. There was no longer a bed for me at the hospital. I had to leave my babies behind and go home without them, which meant I would no longer be able to visit them in the middle of the night. Until now I had been there for every feeding. It was my job. I was their mother. I was supposed to be there for them when they needed me.

I would set the alarm on my cell phone and hobble down the infinitely long hallway to the NICU, my fresh incision burning the entire way. After I scrubbed all my dangerous germs away, I would pick which daughter I was going to feed. A nurse would feed my other little girl in order to keep them on the same rotating schedule. Before I left, I promised the "nurse's" baby that I would feed her the next time. I alternated my babies and it was heart wrenching.

The load of weight on my shoulders was intense, but the guilt was almost unbearable when I was forced to sleep at home. Now I had to settle for only two feedings a day. The only upside to this was that I was able to spend time with Gabriel again. I had missed him so much, and he had really missed me. After I spent the morning with my sweet son, one of his grandparents would come to babysit. The other grandparent would take me to the hospital since I wasn't allowed to drive for two weeks due to my c-section.

We would arrive at the NICU just in time for the noon feeding. From that moment on we were slaves to the clock for the rest of the day. Thankfully the girls had been dismissed from the critical care room the day before I went home. This gave us hope their conditions were improving, and now their incubators could be together in a corner of their new room. Finally, we could visit both babies at the same time. After we fed them, I changed their diapers. We could then cuddle them until one o'clock. They were only allowed outside of their incubators for one hour since they were still unable to maintain their own body heat. After we put them away, we ran downstairs to eat a quick lunch. Upon returning, we sat and watched them rest in their boxes. At three o'clock, we switched babies and repeated the feeding and diaper changing process. After putting them away at four o'clock, I had to say goodbye to my baby girls. I could only hold each of them one time a day, and it wasn't nearly enough. As the elevator doors closed, the shame I felt from leaving them behind was debilitating.

We returned home just as Craig got off work. He picked up the grandparent who hadn't gotten to visit earlier in the day, and the two of them would go to the hospital to cover the girls' six o'clock feeding while I spent my time with Gabe. Craig returned home at eight o'clock and attempted to cram in some quality time with his son. We put Gabe to bed at nine o'clock, and collapsed into bed ourselves just minutes later. We were spread so thin that it made chemo and pregnancy seem like a breeze.

Finally, on day nine, Taylor Moneen Myers was granted permission to come home! She had successfully maintained her own body temperature for twenty-four straight hours. She had proven the doctors right: she was a fighter.

It was bittersweet when we received this great news because it meant that we had to leave Sydney behind at the hospital all by herself. She still wasn't eating consistently, and they wanted to continue to monitor her nutritional intake, or lack thereof.

Exiting the NICU with Taylor in our arms while we were forced to leave Sydney behind was one of the most difficult moments of our entire experience in the hospital. It was so much more comforting when we knew they were there together. We couldn't help but wonder if Sydney would suffer without her sister. I was so worried that she would misunderstand why we left her, and I was desperate for her to know that we loved her just as much as Taylor. We tried to rationalize that she was too little to know any better, but our breaking hearts were telling us a different story. We could only hope we weren't causing permanent, emotional damage to our sweet little baby girl.

The bright side of the situation was that I was afforded a trial run of what it was like to have an infant again. While it was so nice to be able to cuddle Taylor and kiss her any time I wanted, Sydney was still on my mind every moment. In fact, in order to feel better about leaving Sydney behind, I reserved my favorite white bassinette for her arrival. I needed to prove to

80

her that I loved her just as much as Taylor, even though Taylor got to come home first.

On day twelve, Sydney Adair Myers was finally strong enough to come home with us. We were euphoric to leave the NICU behind once and for all! As the elevator descended with Sydney in my arms, I floated with liberation. The sun was beginning to shine in our lives again and I couldn't help but smile.

Did both girls still have a long way to go? Yes. Did we still have a ton of doctor's appointments in our future? Sure. Was there still the looming cloud that since they were preemies they may experience more developmental obstacles? Absolutely. But none of that mattered as long as we could deal with whatever the future might hold together as a family.

Our sweet daughters finally got to meet their dog Tucker, Gabe was quick to show off his choo-choo trains, and Memom could start saving her money to buy her grandaughters anything they wanted. Our girls were home and our family was complete.

It was surreal that night to tuck them in side-by-side in the comfort of their own nursery room. To see them together again was exhilarating. After all we had been through, they were safe and snuggled in their own beds with no attached wires or beeping monitors. For the first time since they were born, they looked content. Gratitude filled our hearts.

Chapter 12: Adjustments

I remember the first moment I considered the possibility of writing a memoir. I was on an airplane flying to my best friend's wedding shower. I had purchased the book "Marley and Me" at the airport bookstore to read during the flight. Obviously I was traveling alone. Had the kids been with me, there would have been no need for reading material because I would have been too busy keeping them occupied.

While I found John Grogan's tales of his troublesome dog to be cute and funny, I couldn't help but draw a parallel between the crazy chaos Marley created for his owners and the unpredictable madhouse we lived in with the twins. I found myself belittling the Grogans' struggles with their pet. I didn't have the luxury of caging my daughters when I needed a break. I would have been arrested for locking them in the garage when they were naughty. I had no choice but to allow them on the furniture, and it was illegal for me to leave them home alone. At the end of a tough day, finding them a better place to live was not an option. Not only did we have one Marley, we had two; and we were stuck with them.

For a while, we deprecatingly referred to our children as Katrina, Wilma, and Hugo since our house felt like the eye of a massive hurricane. Our only choice was to weather the storm and try to come out in one piece. I was forced to jump into survival mode. I learned to appreciate the few good days in which it felt as though the storm was temporarily receding. However, the majority of the time I felt as though I was drowning in toddler and infant madness. I just held my breath and prayed for calmer water.

Gabe was only twenty-five months old when his sisters invaded his life. The peaceful environment he had been accustomed to immediately flipped upside-down when his twins moved in. He made this painfully obvious the day we brought Sydney home. At the sight of his second sister, he pulled his pants down, squatted and deliberately pooped on the floor as he glowered at us. He was already potty-trained, so it was apparent that he was making a bold statement about the newest additions to our family.

In hindsight, Gabriel was the first to recognize how difficult it was going to be for all of us to stay afloat. The girls were more tiring and more work than I could have ever imagined. They were helpless little babies that needed me in order to survive, and it certainly wasn't their fault there were two of them. Even though it was impossible for me to be in three places at once, it was my job to provide a healthy balance for all three of our children.

Every morning at the sound of the first cry, I took a deep breath and said a silent prayer for patience. I gave myself a pep talk as I climbed out of bed and put on a brave and happy face for my first needy child of the day. It didn't matter if I was still exhausted from the day before. Today was a new day, and they were going to need just as much from me today as they did yesterday.

I was tired. Wow! Because the girls drank breast milk for the first six weeks as promised, they ate at least twice during the night. I would wake up, pump, go to the nursery, get them out, place them in their infant carriers, stick a bottle in each mouth, burp them, change both diapers and pray that they would both go back to sleep right away. It was like an assembly line, and it was very impersonal because each night I tried to do it in record time. There was no cuddling, no whispering sweet nothings into their ears, no bonding, and no rocking them back to sleep. It was a job. And it had to be done efficiently so the entire night was not disrupted.

The only way to stay sane was to keep them on the same schedule; otherwise I could have potentially been up all night alternating feedings. So if one girl woke up hungry, I would wake the second one up and make her eat then, too. I knew I could not be a good mother to them during the day if I was only getting a couple of hours of sleep at night. Even though it was not ideal, I had to sacrifice the nighttime nurturing for daytime sanity.

Emotionally, this period was very hard for me. For much of the first year, I was haunted with an amazing amount of self-inflicted guilt. Caring for the girls was so much work I rarely had time to just sit and enjoy them. In the moments I did get to cuddle with one of them, inevitably it was interrupted by the needs of her sister. I was forever putting down a happy baby to tend to a distressed baby. It didn't seem fair to any of us.

The majority of my time was spent feeding them, changing their diapers, giving them baths, doing their laundry, preparing their food for the next day, cleaning up after them and performing other "servicing" chores that were necessary to care for them properly. All the while, I also had to attend to my two-year-old son's needs .

Thankfully, he was a very easy to entertain little kid. For example, Gabriel learned his alphabet by helping me work crossword puzzles while the girls took their morning naps. While I would have *loved* to nap with them every morning, having a two-year-old made that impossible. Still, I had to have *some* downtime in order to recharge my battery for the next portion of the day. As a compromise, Gabe would sit on my lap at the breakfast table and help me fill in the crossword puzzle boxes with the

84

appropriate letters. At first, I would say each letter aloud. His job was to repeat the letter name as I wrote it. Eventually, he could recite the letters on his own as I wrote them. By the time he was three, I could dictate the letters to him while pointing to the appropriate box, and he could write them in the blanks himself.

Working the crosswords with Gabe was beneficial for both of us. Gabriel's knowledge was growing and developing, and I was relaxing at the same time. We both looked forward to our morning crossword puzzle time. He was getting the one-on-one attention he craved from me, and I was able to perform a task that could be left unfinished without affecting the outcome of the day in a negative way. That it self felt liberating.

Every minute I was awake, one or more of my children needed me. I had absolutely no downtime. I was in constant motion while providing for them. While that alone was exhausting, I was running on very little sleep, and I rarely had time to eat a full meal. Inevitably, after a few bites someone would cry or need a diaper change or need a new battery in Thomas the Tank Engine. I had no choice but to abandon my food and continue on in mommy-mode.

With all the constant action, I am sorry to admit that I don't remember very many specifics of the girls' first year. Even when I try to pull memories from deep in the bank, it's just one big blur. Most days were spent going through the motions of care taking, trying to stay afloat the best I could. What I do remember vividly is that it was hard. It was a constant test of patience. More often than not, I made it through the day with the kids with a smile on my face. I had no choice. I was their Mommy.

Even though I appeared to be Super Mom to the kids, I certainly was not Super Wife. I was not good at bottling up the daily stresses associated with the needs of the kids, and, unfortunately, Craig was forced to bear the brunt of it. By the time he returned home from work at the end of every day my patience was depleted and running on reserve. As a result, he became my instant shooting target. I was awful to him. I nagged. I nitpicked. I bitched. I complained. For him, I had run out of smiles.

I expected him to know exactly what to do to care for the kids. Furthermore, I thought he should readily volunteer his services whenever he was available. Even though he was very receptive to doing anything I asked of him, I was resentful that I had to ask at all. Could he not smell their stinky diapers? Did he forget they had to be fed regularly? Was it too much to assume he would volunteer to get up with them on the weekends to offer me a break? Begrudgingly, I would clench my jaw and ask for help. But even then he couldn't perform the task to my standards. I had developed a routine way of doing things so I could maintain some order in my life, and I didn't want him to deviate from my methods in any way. When he did, I assumed he was being lazy. What I really wanted was a clone of myself that could read my mind and replicate my actions. There was no way Craig could live up to these expectations. I was setting him up to fail. Shamefully, I knew that I was behaving inappropriately, but I couldn't help myself.

In spite of all this, he would try to hug me to offer me comfort. He recognized how difficult my job was, and he was trying his best to remain understanding. The last thing I wanted was for him to touch me. Both girls needed to be held all day long, and Gabe happily climbed all over me constantly. I couldn't bear for one more person to invade my personal space.

I took all of my frustrations and aggressions out on Craig because I knew that I could. My security blanket weakened my armor of patience. When he was near I felt safe speaking to him the way I wished I could speak to the kids. While it was a backwards compliment as to how much I trusted him, it was unrealistic for me to think he would see it this way. Because of my temper tantrums and unwillingness to let him touch me, Craig and I were struggling to keep our marriage together. We both felt trapped by our children, even though we loved them dearly.

Finally, when the girls were eight months old, he couldn't take it anymore.

"I'm home!" he announced, as he walked through the door after a long day at work.

"We're in here," I grumbled from the breakfast nook.

Gabe was having a snack and the girls were hanging out in their pack n' play. I was still in my pajamas from the night before and had just barely made it through another day.

"Guess what?" he asked as he threw something down on the table in front of me.

"What?" I asked rhetorically.

"I earned a free trip to St. Thomas!" he bragged proudly, while pointing to the tropical brochure in front of me.

"Good for you," I responded while rolling my eyes.

"That's it?" he asked, offended by my unwillingness to share in his excitement.

"Well it's not like we're going to be able to go, Craig," I pointed out sarcastically.

"Why not, Kristin?" he countered with frustration.

"Gee, let me think," I sassed, while gesturing towards all three of our kids.

"Well, here is how I see it," he announced as he threw his suit jacket over the chair. I didn't even bother to look at him. The thought of us vacationing to an island in the Caribbean was so ridiculous that I wasn't even going to pretend to entertain his deluded fantasies. Those luxuries were for people who didn't have three young children under the age of two to take care of.

"We have two options, Kristin," he declared as he rolled up his shirtsleeves.

"Oh yeah?" I humored him.

"Option One," he announced. "We can leave the kids with your mom, and we can go on vacation together and enjoy ourselves for a change."

"Or?" I dared him with great condescension.

"Or we can go with Option Two," he answered.

"Which is?" I asked, pretending to be bored.

"We can leave the kids with your mom, and we can go visit a divorce attorney," he said with icy seriousness.

Option Two certainly got my attention. I snapped my head up to look at him. I could tell by the look in his eyes that he wasn't kidding.

"We can't live like this anymore, Kristin," he scolded me. "These kids are consuming our lives and it's time we treat ourselves to some fun."

"Are you serious?" I asked, still shocked that he had assumed such control of the situation.

"Do I look like I'm kidding?" he asked.

88

I knew he wasn't. I knew he'd had enough, and I couldn't blame him.

"Well," I said, as I shrugged my shoulders in defeat, "Then I pick Option One."

It was the best thing he could have done for me, and it's certainly the best thing he's ever done for us. Three days into our trip, I was holding his hand as we walked down the curved cement pathway to the beach. In the midst of a light bulb moment, I looked up at him and admitted, "I honestly can't think of *one* thing to be mad at you about right now."

He threw his head back and laughed. "See, babe? You don't hate me," he proved his point. "It's the *kids* that are making you crazy!" he blurted while shaking his hands in the air with overdramatic frustration.

I smiled back at him and conceded, "You might be right."

Right then and there, I realized that the kids were getting to me more than I wanted to admit. I didn't hate Craig at all. In fact, I thought he was cute and funny. He was not an awful husband. He was an amazing one. He was not an incompetent Dad, he was just a guy doing the very best he could to figure it all out.

Could he have proactively done more to be helpful? Yes. Did he know what to do without having to be told and sometimes choose not to - lots of times. Could he have not fallen asleep while holding a baby during the weekend nighttime feedings? I believe so, but he was holding on for dear life to survive the five of us just as much as I was.

He was not perfect, but I certainly wasn't either. I was using him as my punching bag because I had no other outlet. It was wrong and unacceptable. Something had to change, because I did not want to lose the one man that loved me even when I was stir-crazy.

"You know I love you, right?" I asked him.

"Yeah, I know you love me," he answered.

"Do you still love me?" I flirted with him.

"Yeah, I still love you," he flirted back as he leaned down to kiss me on the top of my head.

"Good," I said. "Then I better get my act together, because I'm pretty sure if you leave me no one else would touch me with all these kids," I joked.

He raised his eyebrows, shook his head from side to side and exhaled loudly. "I'm going to have to agree with you on that one!" he admitted honestly.

It was so true that I didn't even take it as an insult. Our kids presented us with a crazy family dynamic; there was no denying that. Just as I had feared in the NICU, my children had consumed me. There was nothing left of me. I was suffocating and it was tearing our marriage apart. It was time for me to admit that I could not do it alone. Even if I could have handled the kids, I would have lost my husband in the process. Not a risk I was willing to take.

The day we returned home, I hired a babysitter to come every Tuesday and Thursday morning. Most of the time, I would leave the house. I would go grocery shopping, get my hair done, go out to breakfast by myself...whatever. When I didn't have any place to go, I would sneak up to my bedroom without the kids knowing and take a long deserved nap.

Having just a few hours a week to myself made the biggest difference in the world. I rediscovered me. I remembered that I was a lot of fun when my children weren't pulling me in a million directions. In those parenting moments when I thought I might yank my hair out, I had Tuesday and Thursday mornings as my incentive to make a graceful recovery.

I was refreshed as a mother, and had learned it was just as important to be renewed as a wife. As result, we also hired a sitter one evening every week. This date-night with my husband became my favorite pastime. As we laughed together over dinner, I was hopeful that someday these fun meals could include the kids. But until then, this allowed Craig and I to remember how much we still enjoyed each other's company.

Chapter 13: Bonding with the Girls...or Not.

Had Taylor and Sydney been singletons, I could have classified each one of them as an easy baby. Since there were two to pacify at the same time, the term "easy" was never considered. At best, systematic was a more appropriate description for my approach to their twin babyhood.

Unlike with Gabriel, I stuck to a very consistent routine with the girls. This was easy to do since we rarely left the house. It was just too difficult for me to take them anywhere alone. Their three temperaments aside, lugging around two heavy infant carriers while keeping track of my two-year-old was more than I could handle with any sense of dignity. As a result, they napped at naptime, they ate at the allotted feeding times, and slept through the night before they were six months old. Thankfully, they were never colicky and they were usually willing to settle with food, a fresh diaper, a blanket, or each other. Aside from meeting their basic needs, they didn't demand too much of me. Physically, this was a blessing since there was only one of me to spread amongst the three of them.

Emotionally, however, it was tougher to swallow. I coveted their adoration and longed for their undivided attention. I was desperate for their affection because I wanted them to need my love the same way Gabriel had. While I had more than enough love to offer each of them, they didn't seem to care. They had already fallen in love with each other, and there was no room for me in the crib.

I knew they liked me well enough, but I wanted more. I wanted to see their eyes light up when I walked into the room. I wanted to feel the electricity of their love as I held them close. I tried so hard to penetrate their intense bond in order to connect with them emotionally. I was glad that they were so content with each other, but I was also jealous that they weren't just as comforted by me. Neither Sydney nor Taylor depended on me for cuddling, loving or nurturing. Instead, they looked solely to each other when those emotions needed fulfilling.

Even when I tried to force them to cuddle with me, they were usually not the least bit interested. I would have loved to rock them to sleep as I had done with Gabriel. When I tried, it only resulted with a stiff arm from whichever twin I was holding. She would spend the entire time with her head pulled away from my chest in a desperate search for her sister. Only on a few occasions was one of them ever pacified enough to be rocked to sleep, and it was never by me. I remember this clearly because my feelings were so hurt by my daughters' unwillingness to allow me to comfort them.

As a general rule, their only sleep requirement was to be next to each other. While they greatly appreciated their thumbs and their favorite blankies, it was the simple presence of her twin that made it possible for either girl to relax enough to fall asleep. Since their cribs were on opposite sides of the room, they both started to develop flat spots on the sides of their heads because they fell asleep gazing at each other. In order to avoid them having lop-sided heads, I had to alternate their directional position at bedtime so their little heads would round back out. For example, if their heads were at the top of the cribs on Monday, I repositioned them on Tuesday so their heads were at the bottom of the cribs.

Not only could I not serve as their security blankets, they also did not allow me any soothing credentials either. In the event that one of them got hurt or angry, I was hopeless to settle them on my own. As any mother

94

would do when her children were upset, I picked them up and attempted to make them feel better. I would hug them, kiss them, and offer tokens of affection and words of comfort and experience no success. In fact, if I held them too long, they cried harder and got angrier. The only thing I could do to make the upset twin feel better was to act as a simple mode of transportation. The final destination of comfort was always her sister. Taylor had the magical power to calm Sydney, and Sydney had the magical power to calm Taylor. I was like a wizard without a wand and no magic in my bag of tricks.

When one needed soothing, I would lie her down next to her sister so they could touch forehead to forehead. The instant she felt the warmth of her sister's head against her own, the screams quieted and the tears stopped flowing. It really was amazing to see. Sometimes, when we knew it was nothing more than a temper tantrum, we would experiment with their twin-spots. We would lay them close to each other, but not touching. Inevitably, the crying baby would wriggle herself toward her sister until she could touch her forehead with her own. Finally, she would calm down.

As time went on, I got smart and discovered a way to fool them. When I wanted to offer comfort to an upset twin, I took her to an entirely different room so that she couldn't see her sister. After placing her on her back, I would then lie down with the top of my head adjacent to the top of her head, our feet outstretched in opposite directions. From above I would sneak my forehead down to rest on top of her forehead, being careful that she couldn't see my face. And while my touch never pacified her as quickly as her sister's did, she would allow herself to give in since I appeared to be the only option. But, in reality, I knew it was the touch of her sister that she

95

was ultimately craving. Eventually, they both conceded enough to allow me the small pleasure of being able to place the palm of my hand on their foreheads in order to help ease their discomfort.

This small victory still felt like defeat. Even though it was phenomenal to witness the intense, innate bond they shared, I couldn't help but feel left out. I was a slave to them every day and every night. I provided them with food, shelter, warmth, and hygiene. I played with them. I talked to them. I sang to them. I tried to do everything with them that I had done with Gabe. Yet it didn't seem to be enough for them to care to connect with me. I couldn't help but feel resentful that they were unwilling to let me share in their snuggles, cuddles, smiles and giggles. These special rewards they had reserved only for each other. No matter how hard I tried, I could not be part of the bond the girls had been building together since conception because I was thirty-four weeks late to the party. Quite honestly, this made me sad and jealous.

Even though I knew this was crazy thinking, it was the truth and I didn't know how to make any sense of it. Because Gabriel had undoubtedly chosen me as the center of his universe during his babyhood, I couldn't help but wonder what I was doing wrong. Why didn't my sweet little girls love me the same way he did? Was it because of the time they spent in the NICU? Did I miss out on my chance to bond with them those first few weeks when they were forced to fight for their lives alone in the incubators? Was it because I fed them in their infant carriers instead of holding them in the middle of the night? Was it because I didn't have enough time to offer as much love and affection as they needed from me? While I knew there were no definitive answers to these questions, I kept asking them over and over again.

As if this didn't haunt me enough, there were moments that I actually felt closer to one twin than the other. Perhaps it was because she had given me a few precious giggles in a row, or smiled when I walked into the room. At the hope of a bond beginning to form, I would latch on to her and feel more attracted to her than her sister. Just as I would start to experience the guilt associated with the uncontrollable sense of favoritism for one daughter over the other, the bond would disappear.

It seemed like it was a game they shared, the other twin would begin teasing me with her own endearing signals that led me to believe I had a fighting chance of being rewarded with her love. The seemingly endless cycle of hope and guilt would be followed just as quickly with rejection. They bounced my heart back and forth like a tennis ball. Eventually I hoped they would accept my unconditional love just as much as the love they felt for the other twin. I was willing to undergo whatever initiation process was necessary in order to become an active member of their club. For now, the maximum occupancy of membership was limited at two.

Chapter 14: SydneyRella and TaylorBell

When Sydney and Taylor were born, it was during the hype of the "Mary Kate and Ashley Olsen 18th Birthday Countdown" on the Internet. Mary Kate and Ashley are beautiful, celebrity, fraternal twins that appear to be identical. They spent much of their careers sharing roles in which they substituted for each other as the same character, unbeknownst to the audience. Because the press focused on the fact that they looked so much alike, it created skepticism about what really constitutes the validity of identical twins. Just looking alike obviously was not the answer.

On many occasions, we felt as though we were being interrogated when the subject of their identical nature would arise.

"Wow! They look exactly alike! Are they identical?" someone would ask.

"Yes," we, *their parents*, would offer our answer of known truth. We were the ones who saw only one placenta during all of their ultrasounds. We were present at their birth when the doctor told us they were identical. We were the parents who had already mixed their daughters up on more than one occasion because their physical characteristics were impossible to distinguish at times. Taking all this into consideration, we felt confident that we were qualified to answer this basic question regarding our daughters. None of this ever seemed to register or make a difference to our ever-cynical audience though, so the next question asked was always the same.

"Are you sure?" we were rudely questioned.

Hmmmmm...let us think about that. "Yes," we answered again, as we plastered on a fake, disgusted smile, raised our eyebrows with annoyed impatience, and nodded our heads with intended condescension.

Yet, still, it never seemed to be enough for these super sleuths. "Well, you know, they could be like Mary Kate and Ashley," the cynics would continue to challenge us.

Because I got tired of offering an explanation in order to prove the girls' case, I decided to take the easy way out. Since we obviously weren't going to beat our skeptics, we decided to join them. As a result, I sent in for an online DNA test. When the test arrived, I swabbed the girls' cheeks myself, sent their samples back to the company, and awaited the results that we already knew. Four weeks and forty dollars later, we received the official documentation that our daughters were, indeed, 99.99999999% identical. Surprise. Surprise.

"We tested their DNA," we could now claim to satisfy our cynical crowd. This seemed to be the reassurance that the Mary Kate and Ashley fans needed before being able to move on with life.

"Ooooh," they would finally concede, while shaking their heads with approval.

Test or no test, to the naked eye the girls were absolutely identical. In fact, I learned to tell them apart much the same way I learned to conduct a science experiment. First, I looked at one girl and made an educated guess. Then I examined her twin sister to test my hypothesis. Finally, I double-checked my results by referring back to the first baby. Only then was I able to identify an accurate conclusion. Often times it was necessary to repeat the process before I felt confident in my decision.

This was especially true when they were infants. During their first three months, they both had very little hair, and no other distinguishing characteristics had yet appeared. The first week they were home, the nurse arrived for the girls' check-up while my mom was in the shower. I went to the nursery and grabbed a baby out of the gray bassinette, whom I naturally assumed to be Taylor since this was the bed she always slept in. As the nurse asked me specific questions regarding Taylor's health, I proudly answered her while I held my sweet little girl in my arms. I kissed her forehead. I picked a flake of dry skin off of her nose. I talked to her and nuzzled her soft cheeks with my own while the nurse recorded my answers and took her vitals. I was reveling in the one-on-one attention that the nurse was compelling me to give to Taylor.

All of a sudden, I heard my mom come running down the stairs. When she realized I was already with the nurse she panicked.

"Kristin, which baby do you have?" she demanded to know.

"Taylor," I responded. "Why?" I asked, picking up on the strange urgency in her voice.

"Because you have Sydney!" she corrected me.

"No, I don't," I said. "I got her out of the gray bassinette."

"I know," my mom explained apologetically. "It's my fault. I put Sydney in the wrong bed. She started crying after I got undressed for my shower, so I hurried and changed her diaper. Then I intentionally put her in Taylor's bassinet because it was closer to the bathroom and I was naked!"

I looked down at my daughter's face with intense scrutiny.

"Are you sure?" I asked incredulously.

"Yes," she said. "I'm sure. You are holding Sydney."

100

Still not convinced, I walked over to the other baby that was lying in the cradle in the kitchen. I inspected her closely, referred back to the one I was currently holding, and then looked back down at her sister again. Sure enough, my mom was right. I was holding, loving, fussing and interacting with Sydney, even though I had no clue it wasn't Taylor! I couldn't believe it!

"Whew!" I said, embarrassed that it had happened in front of the nurse. "That was close!" I admitted.

The nurse was shocked. She didn't even bother to conceal it.

"Oh my goodness! That's never happened before!" she announced. "I guess we'd better start again. Let me grab *Sydney's* file."

In order to avoid confusing them again, we painted Taylor's thumbnails and big toenails bright pink. Why did we pick Taylor? Because her name started with a "T" and so did "Thumb" and "Toe." And when we dressed them in different colors, by default Taylor wore blue, yellow and purple. Why? Because Taylor has an "L" in her name and so do the names of these colors. Sydney got all the colors without an "L": pink, green, red, etc. There was nothing about our identification system that was rocket science, but it was simple to remember and easy to teach to others.

Craig and I could tell the girls apart rather easily by the time they were a couple of months old. But unless you were with them on a consistent daily basis, they were too similar for the unpracticed eye to distinguish. Even though Memom visited quite often to offer her help, it still wasn't enough for her to master their identities. Being the ultra-involved grandmother that she was, this frustrated her to no end. So even though Craig and I were no longer reliant on the nail polish, the first thing Memom did when she came to visit was paint Taylor's thumbs and toes. She was

101

desperate to know them as intimately as she knew Gabriel. Like myself, she wanted them to feel her love and adoration just as he always had. She found it next to impossible to make her granddaughters feel special if she was unable to recognize whom she was holding. She would practice identifying them all weekend long with the help of the nail polish. Usually, by the time she was ready to leave, she had learned to recognize each one individually. However, because babies grow and change so quickly, she would have to start all over with the application of nail polish upon the arrival of her next visit. To say the least, her inability to consistently tell her granddaughters apart drove her crazy.

Memom's dedication and commitment to learning to decipher their identities would be rewarded. Not only did she eventually learn to tell them apart without using any cues, but she also gave her granddaughters their first true gift of self-identification.

When the girls were just a few weeks old, naptime was over. We knew this because, as usual, Taylor was screaming with impatience to gain our attention. Upon hearing her little damsel in distress, Memom quickly ran up the stairs to rescue her. When I reached the nursery, she was already rocking Taylor in an effort to settle her. As it quickly became obvious that Taylor wasn't going to settle easily, Memom offered her to me.

"Should I wake Sydney, too?" my mom asked me, well aware of the fact that I made it a point to keep them on the same schedule.

"Yes," I answered her, with slight hesitation. Even though it ultimately benefitted our entire family to keep their schedules in sync, I always felt guilty for making the decision to wake Sydney when she wasn't done sleeping.

As I was wrestling with this dilemma, I heard my mom address Sydney with loving adoration. "Oh, *SydneyRella!* What a sweet little baby you are!"

Memom had been surprised to discover that Sydney, too, was wide-awake. But, unlike her sister, she was patiently waiting for us to sooth her fussy twin. At the sight of her Memom, Sydney kicked and flailed her arms and legs with delight, thankful for the attention when it came to her.

Since conception, the girls have maintained very different personalities. In my womb, Sydney was passive while Taylor was sure to let her presence be known. Even in the NICU, Sydney rested quietly in her incubator, while her sister was impatient and aggressive. Taylor had even ripped out her own breathing tube when she was all of twelve hours old. After their feedings, Sydney would cooperatively go back to her incubator without any complaint, while Taylor was sure to put up a fight every time, kicking and screaming to express her displeasure. Taylor was so feisty in the NICU that the nurses made jokes about her.

"Don't mess with Taylor!" they would tease light-heartedly. "She doesn't take no for an answer! When she's not happy, we all know about it."

So when Memom christened Sydney with the nickname of SydneyRella that day, it suited her perfectly. She was patient and innately kind. She was passively cooperative, almost to a fault. She didn't demand extra attention, and she was willing to make personal sacrifices in order to make others around her happy. If any baby could ever parallel Disney's Cinderella, it was Sydney. She even had the temperamental, melodramatic sister to prove it!

As time went on and the name stuck, it often got shortened to Rella. Eventually, we called her Rella all the time because Taylor's boisterous tantrums were constantly highlighting Sydney's calm disposition. We noticed that she responded more readily to Rella than she did Sydney. It was obvious she loved having her own special pet name.

We tried to come up with a nickname for Taylor with the intention of keeping things fair, but had trouble getting one to stick. Then one day, I snuck into their nursery just as Taylor was waking up from her nap. When she opened her eyes and found me waiting on her, she was tickled with delight. She panted with excitement, grinned from ear to ear and flailed her little fists with joy. This was a far cry (no pun intended!) from her usual post-naptime screaming routine that occurred when I wasn't instantly at her service. As I picked her up, I couldn't help but laugh at her. She was such a little drama queen!

"Come here, Miss TaylorBell," I said, with a sarcastic tone.

I had never called her that before, but it popped out naturally because my own mom used to call me "Krist-a-bell" as a child. The moment it rolled off my tongue, though, I knew it was a name that was going to stick.

It was perfectly clear: Taylor was Tinkerbell! She was a tiny little sprite packed full of feist. She was extremely spirited and animated, and displayed her emotions for the entire world to see. Her dimple was as magical as pixie dust, and she used it to her advantage by the time she was three months old. She was the life of the party as long as everything was going her way. In the instant she felt deprived of attention, she'd throw a temper tantrum in an attempt to regain the spotlight. Just as when Tinkerbell had Peter Pan's undivided attention, she was contagiously fun; but when Pan was distracted by Wendy, she pulled any ornery stunt necessary to regain his focus. Taylor mimicked Tink so closely it was as if she'd performed a thorough character study!

As the girls got older, everyone was curious about their personalities. They looked exactly alike, so people wanted to know if they acted alike, too. I found that the easiest and most accurate way to answer to this question, without going into great detail in front of the girls, was to offer the monikers they had earned as tiny babies: SydneyRella and TaylorBell. Anything anyone knew about these two Disney characters applied to our girls respectively; both the positive and negative qualities of each.

We had no way of knowing these nicknames would allow Taylor and Sydney to discover themselves as individuals. When they were eighteen months old, we took the girls to Disney World to meet their namesakes. Prior to this vacation, the girls had been content in their own, conjoint bubble. They were always together and, for the most part, had all the same likes and dislikes. Neither one had latched on to anything that was "special" to them, like Gabe had done with Thomas the Tank Engine. Actually, they hadn't shown much interest in anything other than each other.

Rella and T-Bell were sweet and fun little girls, but they were trapped in their own twin world, and had not yet begun to talk to us. At best, they would mimic very basic sounds when I practiced with them. They made no attempt to verbally communicate with the outside world. Instead they contentedly babbled with each other in their own little twin-talk.

In public places, they had never shown any preference as to where we were going or what was on the agenda. To them, going to Chuck E. Cheese was not that different from going to the library. No matter what their environment, they rode together in the stroller seemingly content just to be along. They didn't grab for things while shopping, and they offered absolutely no input on clothing selections, either in the store or at home. They coasted through life together, never needing more than each other for complete fulfillment.

The magic of Disney changed all that. Upon entering the Magic Kingdom, the girls were mesmerized. There were so many people! So much to see! So much to do! They gazed in awe with their mouths open and their eyes wide in disbelief at all the activity that was occurring around them. It was amazing to finally see them respond to their surroundings! For once, something outside of their bubble was captivating their attention!

Every time we saw a picture or statue of Cinderella or Tinkerbell, we would stop, point and say, "LOOK!!!! It's SydneyRella!!!" Or, "Oh my GOSH!! It's TaylorBell!!!!"

The girls were so excited that they would giggle, squeal and point along with us! By mid-day, it was no longer necessary for us to find their respective characters for them. At any and all sightings of Cinderella and Tinkerbell, an explosion of bliss would erupt from the stroller. The appropriate twin would stretch her pudgy little arm and index finger out as far as she could reach to be sure that we could revel in her joy, too. To see the girls not only connect with the world around them, but also want to share their experiences with us was absolutely priceless!

That night we stayed until midnight to see the Spectra parade. Even though the girls had to be exhausted, they were so captivated that they barely blinked. SydneyRella waved to Cinderella in her coach, and TaylorBell watched Tinkerbell fly! As if the whole day hadn't already been perfect, upon exiting the park we were passed by another family with a

106

stroller. Tied to that stroller was one, single, bright red balloon. Again the pudgy arms reached out. Again their index fingers extended.

"Boo!" one twin exclaimed.

"Boo!" the other twin followed in her delight.

Craig and I looked at each other in disbelief. They couldn't possibly be saying balloon...could they??

Then, still pointing, they repeated that precious word over and over again, "Boo! Boo!! Boo! Boo!!!"

Their first, real, spontaneous word had finally emerged. Only the magic of Disney was powerful enough to burst through their bubble! We couldn't have been any prouder, and not to mention relieved. Perhaps there was hope for engaging with them after all!

Thanks to Disney, Taylor and Sydney discovered *themselves*. One day after returning home, we went to the mall. Without realizing it, we walked by The Disney Store. All of a sudden, we heard excited commotion coming from the stroller.

"Me, me!!!!" Sydney shouted with delight, patting her chest over and over again with her chubby little hand. She was right. In the window of the Disney Store was a giant picture of Cinderella. She was identifying herself, and it had nothing to do with her sister.

Shortly thereafter, as the winter began to fade in Michigan, we were outside on a warm spring day. A tiny white butterfly fluttered by at the eye-level of the girls. Again, with a ferocious pat to the chest with yet another chubby little hand, Taylor pointed excitedly.

"Me! Meeeee!!!" she shouted with glee. It took me a second before I made the connection that Taylor assumed the little butterfly was Tinkerbell.

107

It was her turn to go solo. That day she arrived as an individual, separate from her sister. Eventually, Taylor would name butterflies "bubba-ME's." It was adorable.

As time went on, the girls' individual identities continued to emerge as they latched on to their favorite characters. *Cinderella* and *Peter Pan* frequented our television almost daily, and as they watched they were entranced with, quite literally, themselves! When shopping in a store, they would go crazy at the sight of either Cinderella or Tinkerbell. Sydney would get excited for Taylor if they happened to find Tink, and Taylor would be tickled for Sydney if Cinderella popped up somewhere unexpectedly. They loved owning their new identities and every spontaneous sighting was thrilling!

SydneyRella and TaylorBell were transformed. After the Disney trip, they were like new little girls. They had discovered their independence and continued to crave it. For example, when picking out their clothes for the day, I would ask them what they wanted to wear. It used to be a rhetorical formality, because before Disney they never had an opinion on the matter.

But now Sydney would assertively respond with a consistent, "Boo-NeeNeeWewwa." (Translation: Blue Cinderella.)

And Taylor would follow suit with, "Een-Peetah-Bay-o." (Translation: Green Peterbell. When watching Peter Pan, she merged Peter's name with Tink's name. As a confused result, she called her favorite character "PeterBell.")

Because it was so exciting to see them grasp hold to their individualities, their wardrobe quickly transformed from pinks and purples to blues and

108

greens. It was upon their direction that they dressed differently from one another now. So even if they wore the same pants, Sydney's shirt would most definitely be blue and Taylor's was guaranteed to be green.

They even introduced themselves as NeeNeeWewwa and PeetahBayo. Strangers thought this was a bit odd, but I loved it! Every time they would say it, I couldn't help but giggle with delight. Early on I would make attempts to offer background information regarding their strange names, but eventually, I didn't feel I needed to provide justification. In their hearts, they *were* Cinderella and Tinkerbell. Who was I to tell them differently?

Chapter 15: Double the Trouble, Double the Fun

Sydney and Taylor have always been in sync, both psychologically and physiologically. As infants they pacified themselves in the same ways by sucking their thumbs and flicking their favorite knit blankets in between their thumbs and index fingers. When I opened one dirty diaper, I could predict a second one from the other baby within minutes. They even cut the same teeth within days of each other. They both agreed that an early bedtime was not necessary; but they also agreed that waking up much too early in the morning was.

Since they have always been very early risers, we were especially thankful for their contented willingness to occupy each other for an hour or so every morning before disturbing the rest of the household. However, while their initial early morning babbles would start off quietly, they eventually worked themselves into hyper frenzies. My Dad dubbed them "The Monkey Jumpers" as their favorite pastime was to clutch on to the vertical slats of their cribs while using their mattresses as trampolines. They stood facing each other and jumped together as high as they could, all the while giggling in between enthusiastic panting. When their picture frames started to rattle on the walls, we would wake to greet them.

Because the girls were premature, the doctors monitored their physical development closely. At their monthly check-ups, it was obvious that both girls were struggling to reach their physical milestones as quickly and easily as other babies their same age. Taylor, who was born first (although only by two minutes,) conquered all of her milestones before her sister. At first this was worrisome, but eventually we learned to trust that Sydney would get there, too, but usually about six weeks after her sister.

Some of the most basic things that we watched Gabe do naturally as a baby took creative support for the girls. For example, when they were learning to sit on their own it was necessary for us to help them strengthen their core muscles. As a result, I propped them up in either end of a shared laundry basket because the magical Baby Bumbo seat had not yet been invented. In order to strengthen their legs, they exercised often and vigorously in their Johnny Jump-Ups. We had two entrances to our kitchen, so they hung suspended from both door casings. They watched each other as they both bounced with zest, becoming extra giddy the higher they jumped and the wilder they swung. Gabe especially loved it when they were in their Jump-Ups. It was one of his favorite games to pretend that their legs were tunnels for his battery-operated Thomas and Friends. They loved this attention from their big brother and often cried when I removed them before they were ready.

They didn't crawl until they were ten and eleven months old, and they didn't walk until they were thirteen and fourteen months old. Their speech was extremely delayed, and the words they did utter were nearly impossible to decipher. They even mispronounced all of their words the exact same way. Even when one twin was introduced to a brand new word without her sister being present, the other would mispronounce that new word the same way without ever having heard the first twin's original mispronunciation.

Before the girls could talk, they communicated without words. They shared certain gestures, facial expressions, and grunts that seemed

111

unrecognizable. They had developed their own language, indulging in conversations to which the outside world was not privy. They engaged in their twin babble all day long. Even though it sounded like nothing more than noise to us, we were always amazed by their ability to execute a plan together.

One day when the girls were a little over eighteen months old, I realized there was something much more serious occurring than simple speech delays. I was upstairs doing the laundry with them. They loved to "help" fold the clothes. Even though their folding and unfolding made more work for me, it was worth it to keep them safely occupied while doing my household chores. Besides, we enjoyed folding clothes together. I realized they were starting to include me in their fun more regularly now, and I was happy to finally be a part of the in-crowd.

Gabriel was busy downstairs playing with his beloved choo-choo trains. When it occurred to me that I hadn't heard from him in a while, I decided to check on him to make sure he was okay.

I walked to the hallway and stood behind the gate at the top of the staircase.

"Gabriel?" I beckoned him, yelling down the stairs.

Taylor had followed me and now stood ever so importantly by my side.

"Bubba?" she called, mimicking the volume and intonation in my voice.

I chuckled down at her. I thought it was cute how she was acting like Mommy's Little Helper. The girls had taken to calling their big brother Bubba, which Craig and I thought was sweet and endearing. It was our assumption that "Bubba" was their baby-talk version of the word "brother."

When Gabriel didn't respond after the first shout, I raised my voice and yelled louder, "*Gabriel???*"

Again, my little mimic copied me, "*Bubba???*"

When he still didn't answer, I became frustrated because I couldn't leave the girls upstairs by themselves. I tried yelling for him one more time in order to avoid the hassle of having to take them both downstairs to look for him.

"GABE!" I yelled with assertive authority so as to really catch his attention.

"BUH!" Taylor yelled with just as much conviction.

I looked down at her in complete shock.

"*Buh??*" I repeated after her, afraid of the hypothesis that had already formed in my head. It couldn't be...

"Taylor," I addressed her as I shrugged my shoulders and opened my arms wide with question. "Where is Gabriel?" I asked playfully.

She looked at me with her arms open wide and mimicked, "Der Bubba?"

"I don't know!" I answered her, pretending to be confused.

She grinned at me as this was one of her favorite games to play.

"Where is Gabe?" I asked her again, pretending to be stumped.

"Dur Buh?" she asked me right back, eagerly awaiting my typical confused response of 'I don't know.'

Oh. My. God. I suddenly realized Bubba wasn't a pet name for their brother. Bubba was their horrific mispronunciation of Gabriel's name! Worse yet, "Buh" was how they said "Gabe"! Their inaccurate pronunciations weren't even remotely representative of the actual words.

113

Yet they shared the same exact mispronunciation. I knew this couldn't be a good sign.

As time went on, I started to discover and decode more of their twin-talk. For example, one time when we were visiting my dad, I was in the bathroom putting on my make-up. I had left the girls in the living room with Nana. They were playing together so nicely when I went upstairs that I was hopeful I could finish getting ready without any interruptions. All of a sudden, I found myself sprinting down the staircase to break up a fight that Nana had not seen coming. As I ran toward them I threatened, "Don't you dare bite your sister!!"

Unfortunately for one of the girls, I was a second too late and she started screaming. Sure enough, one had bitten the other so hard that there were teeth marks to show for it.

"How did you know that was going to happen??" Nana asked, perplexed.

"I heard them yell 'Dai-dai! Dai-dai!' over and over again," I explained. "That means there's a fight about to break out."

I had learned the hard way that "Dai-dai" translated to "Mine" or "My turn." And when I heard it, I knew to break them up quickly, or else! It turned out that Sydney and Taylor were quite the little piranhas. There was a stretch for about three or four months when Sydney's belly and back were covered with teeth mark bruises. Taylor bit Sydney out of frustration, usually over a toy that she wanted from her sister's possession. The pain from the bite distracted Sydney, causing her to drop the coveted toy. Then Taylor would swipe it away for her own enjoyment. Sydney would bite, too; but more often than not, it was in defense of her sister's shark teeth.

Then one day, it switched. Sydney started to be the attacker and Taylor became the defender. This was not unusual, though. For the first twelve months, they switched behaviors quarterly. Every three months they would transform. Because they were constantly together and always learning from one another, it was as if they would study each other's tactics and try them on for size. Every time I was silly enough to declare that Taylor was a more difficult baby, Sydney was sure to go through a naughty spell just to prove me wrong. Her spells never lasted as long as Taylor's, but she always reminded me that there was plenty of spirit in her little body as well. Then another three months later, they would switch again as if they were collaboratively deciding which roles to play.

Finding the best route of discipline for the girls tended to be very challenging for us. I was spanked as a child, and I had no problem spanking my own children when I deemed it necessary. Gabriel learned "1-2-3" followed by a spanking the first day he decided to dangerously stand in his highchair. Our kitchen floor was made of a rough quartz stone. Had he fallen from his chair and hit his head, he could have been killed. I warned him that standing in his highchair was very dangerous and instructed him to sit down several times. He only looked at me and smiled, as if he was testing my will.

When it was obvious that he wasn't going to listen, I said sternly, "Gabriel, if you don't sit down by the time I count to three, Mommy is going to spank you on the bottom."

Because he didn't yet know what it meant to be spanked, I was prepared to spank him for the first time.

"One....Two....Three," I counted matter-of-factly. He continued to smile at me while he flirted with temptation. I walked over to him and smacked his little bottom. At first he was stunned by the spanking he'd just received, and then he started to cry. His diapered butt didn't hurt, but his feelings certainly did. But he knew I meant business, and he didn't stand up again.

The second time he stood in his highchair, Craig happened to be home. I had told him that I started to use 1-2-3 with Gabriel, and that he was responding to it fabulously. So, Craig decided that he would try out the new method.

"Gabriel, if you don't sit down by the time I get to three, you're going to be in big trouble!" he warned.

"Ooonnnne..." Craig started to count.

Gabriel stared at him blankly.

"Twooooooooooo..." Craig drew out this number and looked at me nervously.

Gabe offered Craig a sheepish grin, and shot a daring glance at me.

"Three!" Craig finished counting.

Gabe continued to stand, and it was obvious he had no intention of sitting down. He looked at Craig with a cocky smirk as if to say, "Ha! I win!"

Craig looked at me and asked dumbly, "Now what I do?"

"You spank him," I said, surprised that he didn't already know. Obviously he had only been half-listening to my stories.

"*What?*" he stammered back.

"Craig, don't count unless you plan on following through!" I lectured him. "You got to three and he ignored you. Now you have to spank him!"

As much as it pained him to do it, Craig picked his little boy up and swatted his bottom. He then sat Gabriel back down in his chair with authority. Gabriel cried briefly, and then it was over. He stayed seated, and we proceeded to share a pleasant family dinner.

That night in bed, Craig rolled over and hugged me.

"I feel *soooo* bad for spanking Gabe tonight," he whined with regret. "If I would have known I was going to have to spank him, I never would have counted!"

"But did it work?" I asked him.

"Yeah," he admitted. "I hate to say it, but it really did work."

After that, all we ever had to do to discipline Gabriel was count. Rarely did he let us get past two. When he did, he received a swift reminder on the bottom. But most often, he opted to stop the bad behavior and chose to behave appropriately instead. The one and only time he bit me, I bit him right back. The pain it caused him made him understand why it was bad, and he never did it again.

He was the easiest kid in the world to discipline. When put in a time-out, he would sit patiently until he was told to get up. One time I actually forgot that I had put him in a time-out. My mom was there and we had gotten immersed in conversation. After twenty some minutes, Memom noticed her sweet grandson sitting quietly in the chair.

Unaware that he had been in trouble, she pondered aloud, "What do you think he's thinking about? He's been sitting in that chair so quietly," she observed.

"Oh, no!" I said startled, as I clutched my hand over my mouth. "He's still in time-out!" I shrieked as I bolted to the time-out chair.

Sure enough, Gabe sat patiently waiting for his time-out to be over. He would never have dreamt of getting up without my permission to do so. After that, Gabe and I agreed that when he was in time-out he was to count to twenty slowly and say his ABC's. After he performed those two tasks, he could get up and, of course, that's just what he did.

None of this was the case, however, with the twins. We constantly struggled to figure out a consistent way of appealing to their consciences. Something would appear to work for a little while, and then like good little antibodies, they became immune to our punishments.

When we spanked them, they would literally laugh in our faces. Time-outs were completely unsuccessful because the twin that wasn't in trouble felt sorry for the naughty twin. To make her sissy feel better, she would sit with her and comfort her throughout the entirety of her punishment. Taking something away from the twin in trouble worked occasionally, but most of the time the other twin offered her something else that appeased her. We tried to reward the "good girl" and ignore the "bad girl," but at the young age of two this really didn't bother them so much. The only discipline technique we had any luck with was to throw away something they loved, like shoes. While this sounds silly, the girls have always loved fancy shoes. Since time-outs and spankings proved to be a waste of time, the only way we could really make our point was to threaten to throw away their favorite pairs of shoes. They would scream and cry and yell, "NO, NO, NO!!!" as they saw their shoes heading towards the trash. If there was anything that would end their bad behavior, this was it.

In reality, what we discovered is that they didn't mind getting into trouble because they always had a partner in crime. While we understood the logic behind this, it was infuriating to us as their parents who were supposed to be the authority figures. To them, the punishment was always a small price to pay for the fun and excitement they shared while committing the crime.

And, oh, the crimes our two little girls have committed....

Chapter 16: Left...Right?

Just as their personalities developed over time, there were slight physical developments that started to distinguish the girls from one another along the way as well. For example, Taylor has a dimple when she smiles and Sydney does not. As their hair grew in, it became obvious that Taylor's natural part was on the left side of her head, and Sydney's natural part was on her right side. As they fell in love with their thumbs as pacifiers, it was always true that Sydney only sucked her right thumb and Taylor only sucked her left thumb. Conveniently enough, both of these facts adhered to the "L" rule, so it was easy for us to remember! Eventually, we would determine that Taylor is left-handed and Sydney is right-handed. All of this led to the conclusion that, not only are the girls identical, but they are also mirror image twins. This means they are transversely the opposite across the midline.

Spatially their right and left sides proved to be very important too, as I discovered when they were two and a half. We moved into our new house and had left their cribs behind. It was time for them to transition into their big girl beds, and they were really excited!

On the left side of their shared bedroom, Taylor's monogram "TMM" was hot-glued to the shelf above her bed that housed her beloved Tinkerbell collection. Hanging on her bedside wall were pictures of her dressed as Tinkerbell. Adversely, Sydney's bed, her own hot-glued monogram "SMA", her Cinderella collection, and pictures of her dressed as Cinderella all decorated the right side of the room. I was proud of how I had created space that suited them both within the same room.

The girls were tickled with delight when they saw their favorite Disney character decorations adorning their room, and they took great pride in showing off their big girl beds to whoever would listen. However, when it was time to go to sleep, their attitudes told a very different story. It appeared their fancy beds were for bragging rights only, because they refused to sleep in them. For a week straight we fought them to stay in their beds. It seemed the only way they would fall asleep was if they were together on the floor, but this was unusual because they had always slept in separate beds. Every night at bedtime they went to work throwing their pillows and blankets in the middle of the floor. They nestled in side-by-side and waited for us to tuck them in. Mistakenly, we attributed their floor sleeping as a means of adjusting to the move. We assumed they felt insecure in their new environment, and found solace in each other's presence. We reasoned that, surely, this would pass as they grew acquainted with our new home.

It didn't pass. No matter what we did, we could not get them off the floor. More than a month later, I was struggling to get them to take their naps, which was not at all uncommon. I left the room frustrated with defeat. Again, they had refused to sleep in their beds. This combined with the usual; I couldn't get them to keep their hands to themselves. Their close proximity on the floor was consistently making naptime and bedtime impossible. Instead of sleeping, they messed around tickling, patting, hitting, pulling hair, etc. Going to bed turned into slaphappy distraction games for them, and utter dread for us. We entered the ritual knowing it was going to be a long, exhausting and infuriating process. Craig resorted to lying guard

121

outside their bedroom door for hours at a time in order to intimidate them enough to sleep.

On this particular day, as I was failing again to put them down for their naps, I distanced myself from them in the hopes of maintaining control of my temper. I plodded down the stairs and pouted at the kitchen table. I was exasperated. Unwelcome tears surfaced as my emotions unraveled. Naptime was making me crazy, but none of us could afford to give it up. They still needed their naps for the sake of getting enough rest. Actually, I still needed them to nap to maintain my sanity. A mental break from them during the day was not yet an option, but rather a necessity.

I had to get them to sleep in their beds. They couldn't relax and unwind unless they were separated. Before our house was completed, we had temporarily lived at my mom's lake house while it was vacant for the winter. While we were there, they slept in twin beds and never once asked to go to the floor. I couldn't help but wonder why they would agree to sleep in beds there, but not at our house? What was different? There had to be a logical explanation for their odd behavior. What was *really* going on? Was it possible they were just *bad* little girls?

I gritted my teeth in fear of that truth. I could feel the onset of yet another tension headache as a result of my clenched jaw. This was a coping mechanism that I had become all too familiar with since the birth of our girls. I closed my eyes, took a deep breath and rubbed my forehead. I imagined them giggling on the floor in their self-made beds. I sneered at the thought of them overtly defying us as they wriggled together in a delighted tangle of arms and legs. The Tinkerbell blanket flung in the air on the right side, as the Cinderella blanket lie tousled in a ball on the left.

Those blankets had become the representation of my worst nightmare: twin daughters that never slept. Those blankets were controlling my life.

"Those blankets!" I reveled with excitement. It was like a light bulb switched on in my head. "Oh my God!" I thought. "That's it!"

They *were* making their beds on the floor for a reason! I sprang from my chair and sprinted upstairs. The answer was so blatantly obvious! Why hadn't I thought of it before? How could I have been so stupid?? We could have saved ourselves from *so* many headaches!!! I was absolutely certain that I had discovered the solution.

"Get up, girls!" I eagerly directed as I barged into their rooms. "You're sleeping in your big girl beds today!!"

Scared by the sudden and frantic disruption, they rebelled in unison, "NO, Momma, NO! Poe, poe!!" (Poe was their word for floor.)

"Don't worry, girls!" I reassured them. "Mommy is going to fix it!!" I announced joyously as I started to tear their room apart like a mad woman. They stood together quietly in the corner, holding on to each other for comfort. They looked at me as though I'd lost my mind, and watched in wonder as I destroyed their room in a glorious frenzy.

I took every picture down from their walls. I stripped their beds and threw their blankets in a pile on the floor. I removed every Tinkerbell and Cinderella collectible off their shelves. And for the grand finale, I yanked their hot-glued monogrammed letters off the wooden shelves with my bare hands.

"I'll be right back, girls!" I sang victoriously as I raced downstairs to fetch the glue gun. When I re-entered the room, they hadn't budged. Their eyes were wide with curiosity as they anxiously anticipated my next move.

"Mommy knows why you won't sleep in your beds!" I announced my brilliant discovery. "They're on the wrong sides, aren't they????"

With their thumbs in their mouths, they both smiled and shook their heads up and down with excited affirmation. I leaned down and squeezed them tightly. The relief I felt was liberating, even though I was sorry I hadn't come to this conclusion earlier.

"Mommy loves you!" I told them sincerely. "Now let's get this cleaned up so you can take your naps!"

While the glue gun was heating, the girls helped me put everything away on the exact opposite sides of the room. If it used to hang on the left, I hung it on the right. I put Sydney's covers on Taylor's bed, and Taylor's covers on Sydney's bed. Tinkerbell moved to her new side of the room, and then Cinderella did the same. I made the switch official by re-gluing their initials on the opposite shelves. In less than half an hour, their entire room had been reversed from left to right.

"Okay!" I sang. "Into your beds you go!"

And that's exactly what they did. Without any hesitation or argument, both of my two-year-olds climbed into their big girl beds. They put their thumbs in their mouths, rolled over and went to sleep. Our problem was solved.

That evening when Craig came home, he was amazed when I told him the story.

"How did you know??" he asked, baffled.

I explained my revelation to him with great excitement.

124

"I don't know why I didn't think of it before!" I admitted with shame. "When I pictured them on the floor, I envisioned Taylor's Tinkerbell blanket on the right side and Sydney's Cinderella blanket on the left."

"Yeah. So?" Craig probed.

"That was constant. They never fought over where their blankets went, even though they were on the wrong sides of the room according to how we had their beds positioned."

I could tell he still wasn't getting it.

"That's when I realized that since *conception* they have had assigned sides in spatial relation to each other. Sydney was on the right side of my belly and Taylor was on the left side. Taylor's bassinette and crib were also positioned to the left of Sydney's bassinette and crib! And this is how they slept at my Mom's, too, which is why they would stay in the beds at her house," I said, irritated that it had taken me this long to put it all together.

"They weren't fighting us because they wanted to sleep *together*," I concluded. "They were fighting to sleep on the correct *sides* of each other!"

"But I thought Taylor was the lefty and Sydney was the righty?" Craig challenged. "Isn't that why we put their beds where we did?" he asked, still confused.

"That's true," I agreed with him. "We decorated their rooms according to our right and our left when looking into their room from the doorway, but when they lie down, their heads are at the opposite end of the room. So, this whole time it's been about perspective. To us, they were on the correct sides, but to them, they were on the wrong sides! They needed to be on *their* right and *their* left...not *our* right and *our* left!"

125

"Wow, babe! What made you think of that?" he asked, thoroughly impressed.

"I don't know," I said. "I guess because I refused to accept that the only reason they were sleeping on the floor was because they were bad."

"Good point," Craig said as he exhaled deeply and rolled his eyes. "But I don't think we should give them too much credit."

"Why? I think they deserve it!" I said protectively.

"Maybe this time," he conceded. "But I *do* think it's fun for them to drive us crazy. It's a conspiracy!"

I didn't argue with this. I laughed and agreed whole-heartedly. The Twin Conspiracy Theory...he was certainly on to something!!

Chapter 17: I'm Grumpy Because You're Dopey.

Honestly, I never knew what to expect. I could never predict, based on the day before, as to whether or not we were going to have a good day or a bad day. Some days were easier than others. When the girls were two years old, it seemed as if every day was nearly impossible. They were full of energy and always eager to brave new adventures together. They worked cooperatively to coordinate their mischief - It was all for one and one for all. What one twin didn't think of, the other twin did. As if that weren't enough, they understood the meaning of stealth mode while sneaking to execute their covert operations.

For example, I now only buy liquid laundry detergent as a result of the day they helped each other scale the washing machine in order to reach the full box of powdered Tide. Once they retrieved it, they proceeded to dump the entire giant sized box all over the laundry room floor. I found them as they were blissfully (and quietly) pretending to ice skate in the enormous mess.

After scolding them, I fixed them some oatmeal for breakfast so they would be sufficiently occupied while I cleaned up the soapy disaster. After completing this very unexpected and annoying morning chore, I walked into the kitchen only to find that they had finger painted the entire surface of the wooden breakfast table with their oatmeal. Then while I scrubbed the dried oatmeal off the table, they seized this opportunity to sneak into my make-up. They loved to put on lipstick: on their face, on their hands, on their bellies, on the counter-top, on the wall.... anywhere. In fact, I finally started keeping my lipstick safely in my purse because they had already figured out how to disable the childproof lock on the drawer that I kept it in.

This is the way it went. They were so fast that I could not keep up with them. They knew I was occupied, and saw it as their opportunity to get into something that they were not supposed to. I spent all day cleaning up their disasters, all the while praying I wouldn't lose my mind.

Little Gabriel learned early on what an "emergency" was. He'd run in to the kitchen while I was busy cooking or cleaning up after a meal and exclaim, "Mommy, there's an emergency!"

Upon hearing these words, I would cringe because inevitably it meant there was a huge twin-induced mess somewhere just waiting to be cleaned up. On one such day, about six weeks after we'd moved into our brand new house, Gabriel came running into the family room declaring yet another emergency. Initially I was confused because I trusted that the girls were napping.

The four of us had spent the morning bravely running errands together. Surprisingly, it had been a very liberating day. All three kids had been extremely well behaved, and we had actually enjoyed our time together. I even took them to McDonald's to celebrate our stress-free freedom from the house. The girls had spent the day taking turns carrying my purse to and from the car, which was a job they took very seriously. My purse was practically bigger than they were, and it took all the strength and coordination they could muster just to keep it on their little shoulders. Because they felt so important while carrying it, it proved to be a positive incentive that they coveted. They took great pride in this big girl task, and they thrived on my willingness to trust them with such an important possession of mine.

When we returned home with our tummies full, the girls willingly marched upstairs for naptime. It was Sydney's turn in the rotation to carry my purse. I giggled as I watched her struggle to carry it up the stairs. She was obviously on a mission. I didn't have the heart to cut her mission short by reminding her that I kept my purse on the first floor. And I didn't want to insult her by offering to help carry the load, so instead I followed at a close distance so I could safely support her independence.

I was so proud of both girls for alternately sharing the task without a single argument all day. It was so refreshing to see them work together for a good cause, rather than only teaming up to create mischief. As I tucked them in for their naps, I praised them for being such good little girls. They smiled brightly and seemed to bask in the positive attention. It seemed as if maybe we had just turned a positive corner in their maturity and development. When I left their room, they were both sleeping soundly and my heart was full of hope.

Little did I know that they had plotted a Twin Plan. When I walked into their room to check on Gabe's rumored emergency, I discovered Sydney and Taylor working together to execute this plan with fierce determination. What I had failed to remember earlier in the day was that I had been "hiding" my red lipstick in my purse. The girls had silently awoken from their naps and launched their stealth mission without a peep.

I found them sitting back-to-back in the center of their brand new ivory carpet inside a four-foot wide, bright red, Bobby Brown lipstick circle. In silent wonder, I watched as Sydney traced over her half of the circle with

129

the lipstick. Then she handed it off to Taylor so that she could complete the arc. They were working together to be bad, and they knew it. When they discovered that I had entered the room, they both stood up and ran to Sydney's bed, desperately trying to hide the lipstick in her brand new white sheet.

My heart sank, and I was numb with defeat. My bubble of hopeful enthusiasm burst into a million pieces. A sick, cold silence filled the room. I could tell by the looks on their faces that for the first time my children were afraid of me. In that moment, I was also afraid of me. I knew if I started yelling, I might never stop. If I started spanking, I might lose control. It was right then that I understood how it was possible for a parent to beat his or her children. Thankfully, I restrained myself, but I did experience a momentary revelation of empathy for those parents who had succumbed to the maddening fury provoked by a naughty child.

The girls didn't say a word. They followed at my heels like puppy dogs as I went to fetch the OxyClean. They lay in their beds completely still as they watched me attempt to scrub the blood-red lipstick off the carpet for a solid hour. I believed they were sorry, but that did nothing to make me feel better. I scrubbed and scrubbed as silent tears fell down my face. My disgust grew every time I looked at them. I felt like a fool for hoping that we were making forward progress. The realization that the cycle of bad behavior was only going to continue fueled my depression. When my arm hurt from scrubbing, I gave up on the stain. I trudged down the stairs to the laundry room and threw away the ruined sheet.

When Craig got home from work that night, I turned them over to him. I still could not look at them without feeling hopelessly broken. He fed them

130

dinner, played with them, and tucked them in to bed. I wallowed in self-pity despite Gabriel's best efforts to comfort me.

I stopped moping long enough to tuck Gabe in that night. I needed to thank him for being such a supportive helper. I apologized for devoting so much of my attention to his naughty twin sisters. As always, he was more than willing to forgive me with hugs and kisses. Gabe's sweet and tender nature made me dare to hope. He was a constant reminder of what the girls were capable of becoming if I could just get them through this *terrible* age of two. He and I were living through the twin madness, and there was nothing we could do but stick it out together.

When I woke up the next morning, I was surprised by how much better I felt after a good night's rest. After feeding the kids breakfast, I decided to tackle the lipstick yet again. I took them upstairs with me and instructed them to read for a little while. The girls have always loved books, so I knew I had about a half-hour to make miracles happen on the carpet.

Because I knew I had a big cleaning job ahead of me that day, I hadn't bothered to shower. Let's face it, lots of days I didn't have time to even get out of my pajamas. I was on the go chasing kids all day long. Taking time to shower meant no supervision for fifteen minutes, and there was no way I was willing to risk the twin damage that could occur in that amount of time! My idyllic vision of what it meant to be a stay-at-home-mom had exploded the moment the twins became mobile. Before, I had been guilty of casting judgment on other stay-at-home-moms who hired the help of a nanny. But I wasn't judging them anymore. Instead, I was envious.

After I finished scrubbing the carpet to the best of my ability, I headed downstairs to throw the rags in the wash. That's when I rediscovered the lipstick stained sheet popping out of the trash. The kids had been very well behaved while I worked on the carpet, so I was rejuvenated and feeling productive. I decided it was at least worth a shot to try to save the sheet. I threw it in my utility sink, turned on the water, and added a hefty amount of bleach. After all, what could it hurt to let it soak?

Just then I heard my doorbell ring. This was strange since our community is gated and all visitors must be announced with a phone call from the security guard. My intention was to peek at our guest from a side window before deciding whether or not to answer the door, but the girls beat me to the punch. There they both stood, waving out the front window with all their might. Now I had no choice but to be cordial.

It still didn't occur to me to be concerned, though. I assumed it was a builder or landscaper coming by to finish the last details of our new house. As I reached to open the door, it was no big deal that my sweaty hair was thrown into a disgusting ponytail on the top of my head. I still didn't care that I was wearing flannel boxer shorts. It didn't yet occur to me to be embarrassed by my gray, puffy painted, bubble lettered T-shirt that read "I'M GRUMPY BECAUSE YOU'RE DOPEY." I had purchased the shirt as a joke during our recent trip to Disney World, and had worn it for the first time the night before in an effort to apologize to Craig for my foul mood after the ill-fated lipstick episode.

When I opened the door, my confidence was derailed by the golden aura of the Louis Vuitton glamour girl standing on my front porch. I had to fight the urge to run and hide. I crossed my arms in front of me as fast as I could, desperate to conceal my trashy t-shirt. I had no idea who this woman was, but I was certain that the unsightly first impression I offered her would not easily be forgotten.

"HHHHiiiiiiiiiiii," I said, suddenly worried as I realized that I faintly recognized her.

"Hi!" said the beauty queen. "I'm so sorry to drop in on you like this. I know it's unbelievably rude of me!"

"Oh, that's okay!" I lied through my teeth as I searched my brain frantically for a positive identification.

"Don't worry!" the mystery woman reassured me. "I don't plan on staying. My driver is waiting on me," she said as she pointed to the *chauffeur* who was waiting by her car. "But I really wanted to drop this off and welcome you to the neighborhood!"

"Oh my gosh! Thank you!" I tried to sound cool as I reached down for the *Louis Vuitton gift bag* that she extended to me.

"We've had it at the house forever," she informed me as she gestured to the house next to ours. "I feel awful that it's taken me this long to get over here!"

Finally it registered. I was speaking to our next-door neighbor. I had met her one time before, but on that particular day her luxurious hair had been pressed straight. Today it was wavy and chic.

I had no choice but to ask to her in, even though I was mortified by the state of my appearance. Instantly I felt the need to explain myself so that she didn't assume the Beverly Hillbillies had just moved in.

"You'll have to forgive my appearance," I attempted to justify. "But we've had a bit of a lipstick catastrophe up in the girls' room, and I've been scrubbing their new carpet all morning!"

I cringed as I gestured at the twins who were standing by my side. They couldn't have looked any grubbier. They were naked except for their crinkled and snagged pull-ups. Their unbrushed hair was as snarled and unkempt as could be. To top it off, their cheeks and bellies were covered with crusty yellow remnants of an egg-yolk breakfast.

"Oh, your girls are so beautiful!" she said kindly.

They were not beautiful in that moment. They were dirty. My uninvited guest was being polite while I was kicking myself for skipping our morning hygiene routine in order to clean the carpet! I was flabbergasted by the irony that, of all mornings, she picked this one to pop in and say hello.

As we continued to make small talk in the foyer, I quietly started to panic as I noticed Taylor tugging at her pull-up.

"Oh Taylor!" I begged her telepathically. "*Please* don't take off your pull-up right now! Please, don't..."

Unfortunately, she didn't hear my non-verbal request. Because before I could even complete my thought, she yanked her pull-up down past her knees and on to her ankles. Not only would I have preferred that my daughter not strip naked in front of our company, but I also knew very well that the only reason the girls ever pulled off their own pull-ups was when they had pooped in them. Everything was happening faster than I could control.

"Please, God," I silently prayed as hard as I could, "don't let her pull-up be full of shit!!!"

134

Well, I quickly discovered that God had more pressing needs to attend to at that moment because about a hundred little turtle-head poopies started to fling out of her diaper.

"No!!!!!" I cried inside. "This cannot be happening!!!!"

Without thinking, I started to dive bare handed for the confetti of turds that surrounded our feet. I was willing to do anything to get the shit off the floor when I realized that my guest might not be very impressed with that method of clean-up. So I turned to Taylor and ripped the pull-up off her little ankles as fast as I could. I turned it inside out and used the crotch of the diaper as a glove. I apologized profusely to my neighbor as I hastily cleaned up the fecal assault, all the while wanting to curl up in a ball and die of embarrassment!

Once I finally got all the little turds picked up, I cringed when I faced her.

"I am so sorry. You just never know what to expect with 2 two-year-olds," I explained to her, regretfully.

She really was trying her best to be sweet and understanding, reassuring me that it was nothing to worry about as she had raised a child, too. Suddenly, though, I noticed that she started to back towards the door with a horror-stricken look on her face.

"Oh, MY" she shrieked, startled. "Is that your *dog*?" she asked the rhetorical question, finally unable to mask the judgmental tone in her voice.

At first, I was confused by her baffled nature. Tucker was the friendliest little cocker spaniel a person could ever want to encounter. He greeted guests with his tail wagging with excitement. Ordinarily, strangers fell instantly in love with him.

135

When I looked down to see what the fuss was about, I was dreadfully reminded of the fact that Tucker had just had a large fatty mass surgically removed from his back the day before. As a result, the entire top right quarter of his back was shaved to the skin and bearing a fresh, raw, six-inch, stitched incision.

I took a deep breath and rolled my eyes. As if it weren't enough that I had already justified my own appearance and my two-year-old's inappropriate display of her bowel movements. Now I had to explain why my dog looked like he just stepped out of a gory movie!

"Yes, that's Tucker. He had a preventative cancer procedure yesterday," I sugarcoated the explanation.

By that point she was done being polite. She already had one foot out the door as she bid farewell. It had to have felt as though she'd entered the parenting Twilight Zone. As she pulled the door shut behind her, I stood stunned by the sequence of events that had just occurred. I was mortified. I was also pissed at Craig for having dodged the bullet! After all, he was the one that wanted to move into this damn neighborhood! It was so unfair that I suffered that embarrassment alone! I headed straight for the phone to complain to him. Before I reached the handset, I heard the faint sound of running water.

"Hmmm....that's strange," I thought to myself. "I wonder where that could be coming from?" When all of a sudden I was blasted by the memory of the bleach water in the utility sink. I had gotten so preoccupied with our unexpected company that I had completely forgotten about the lipstick stained sheet I was trying to save!

"Noooooooooooooooooo!!!!" I screamed out loud as I sprinted toward the laundry room.

I was forced to abruptly stop short when I reached the mudroom. I couldn't believe what I saw. There was an inch of bleach water covering both surfaces of the adjacent mudroom and laundry room floors. Fortunately the water had not yet reached the dark hardwood in the kitchen. Thank God Tucker had entered the foyer when he did, because if my guest had stayed any longer our new kitchen floor would have been destroyed.

So again, the tears fell. Another mess awaited me. It took an hour to soak up all of the water. The ceiling below eventually had to be repaired as a result of the flood. But considering how much water was on the floor, it was minimal.

Since then, every time we have run into our neighbor she has been very forgiving. She even tries to assume responsibility for the mayhem that occurred. She talks about the experience light-heartedly, as if it were no big deal. The blood rushes to my face and my anxiety spikes when she reminisces, "I've told so many people about that day, and have vowed that I will *never* drop by someone's house *ever* again without proper warning!" This is what I had feared all along – a story that would be told over and over again without my cushioned perspective attached.

In retrospect, this was the most chaotic and stressful 24-hours that I've ever experienced. It was also the moment that I knew that I had to write this book. Our twins were providing us with material that couldn't be made up.

Chapter 18: Out of Control

If there was one thing we could count on while raising the twins, it was that the simplest things always turned into chaos. It seemed Chaos was an unwelcome guest that wouldn't take no for an answer. This bully showed up everywhere, even in places you'd least expect.

Pure agitation was incited every time a proud grandma whipped out her camera with the intention of capturing the perfect posed shot of her grandkids. It was tough enough to coerce all three kids to look at the camera at the same time, but to expect them all to smile, too? That was just asinine. Every time I heard the words "Say Cheese!" I wanted to scream. I cursed digital cameras. The instant proof when the picture wasn't perfect was cruel. Every photo-op lasted an eternity, and most often resulted with irritable kids who were tired of smiling, and a crabby mom who was tired of asking them to.

Even pastimes designed to create peace and quiet led to chaos. Take coloring, for example. A crayon war was unavoidable. Even though there were 64 colors in the box, it was a certainty that the girls would need red at the exact same moment.

Reading aloud books carried their own sets of issues. If I read to more than one child at a time, they would fight to turn the pages. When I read to all three kids, they battled over the seating arrangements. The favorite spots were snuggled into the left and right of me. The third one had to squeeze between my spread legs and lean on my chest, which was never as comfortable. As they grew, they suffocated me as I read to them. More than a hundred pounds of their combined weight was draped all over my hundred pound frame. By the time the book was over, I could hardly stand the discomfort.

Even getting Gabriel back and forth to pre-school was a daily ordeal because of the twins. Both girls had to be strapped and unstrapped from their car seats in order to walk him to his classroom. Since I only had two hands for holding on to the girls, Gabe hung on to my back pocket so that I could feel his presence while we safely walked through the parking lot. On the way to his classroom we had to walk through the Gross Motor Gym, which was every toddler's dream. The giant room was full of tricycles, trampolines, playhouses, bouncing ponies, etc. However, it was not open for sibling play because class was in session. I chased Sydney and Taylor off the equipment every day. Often times I'd catch one while the other escaped back to play. Then, before it seemed possible, we'd have to go through the whole process again at pick-up time. No matter what the activity was, I always felt scattered. I was pulled in three different directions, always feeling as though I didn't have enough to give. Simply put, I was outnumbered by my three young children.

Even when they were sleeping on the right sides of the room, the twins' naptime was so consistently dramatic I dreaded it. It was amazing how the girls fought sleep. Never once did they fall asleep in the car. Never once did they fall asleep in their stroller. Never once did they fall asleep while watching TV. It was as if they were terrified of missing out on something if they took the time to nap. The only way they would even consider sleep as an option was if they were in their beds and no other distractions were available.

Because our days operated so much smoother when they were well rested, I was adamant that they continue to take their naps. It took an extreme amount of patience, discipline and follow-through on my end in order for them to succumb to sleep. I hated that I had to act like a drill sergeant in order to get them to cooperate. Getting them to go to sleep almost always left me in a cranky mood with a headache.

One day after I had finally gotten the girls down, I felt guilty that the process had taken longer than usual. Gabe always waited on me patiently, and I was regretting the fact that his needs were always put on hold in order for me to take care of his sisters. In an effort to reward him for his patience that day, I suggested that we race upstairs and read a book together. He was delighted with the challenge of a race and willingly accepted my plan.

"On your mark...*get set*...GO!" I exclaimed enthusiastically.

As usual, I took off with great speed to make him believe that I was trying to win. I heard him giggle behind me as he sprinted joyfully to catch me. I looked over my shoulder to catch a glimpse of his happy little face. I needed to see that reassuring smile as much as he deserved to feel it. All of a sudden, though, things took a horrible turn for the worse.

I saw Gabriel's toe catch on the step that separated the carpeted family room from the ceramic tiled foyer. Like it was in slow motion, his little body flew horizontally through the air. I winced as his chin crashed down onto the hard ceramic floor. I knew it was a treacherous fall. I also knew that, more than likely, his chin was going to be bleeding.

As I ran over to comfort his scream of pain, I am ashamed to admit that the overwhelming fear that was present in my mind had nothing to do with

140

my sweet, injured son. Instead, my mind was consumed with a dreadful prayer.

"Please!" I begged God. "Don't let the cut be so bad that he needs stitches! I just got the girls down for their nap! I *don't* want to wake them up! I *do not* want to take them to the emergency room!" It was true; I was utterly annoyed when I rolled my little boy over to see the long, gaping gash on the bottom of his chin.

"Oh, buddy!" I said to comfort him. "Mommy is so sorry! It's all my fault! I should have never asked you to race!"

My four-year-old boy was sobbing from the throbbing pain as blood exuded from his chin. I hugged him tightly as I prepared myself for the mass amount of chaos that was going to envelop at least the next four hours of my day. I took a deep breath because I knew I was going to have to prepare him as well.

"Gabe, I need you to listen to me, okay?" I said to him in a tone that was not at all nurturing. He looked at me as he continued to cry.

"Honey, I know you want Mommy to take care of you right now. And, believe me, I wish I could. But sweetie, you need to see a doctor so he can fix your boo-boo," I told him as his eyes grew wide with horrific fear.

"Do I need stitches, Mommy?" he asked, scared of my answer.

"Yes you do, buddy," I answered honestly. "But we can't go without the girls. I need you to be brave and lay here by yourself while I wake them up and load them into the car," I said regretfully as I took his little hand and showed him how to hold the towel I had grabbed from the adjacent powder room on his chin. He looked at me like I was crazy.

"Mommy! I want you!" he pleaded as alligator tears flooded his face.

"I know, Gabriel, but that's not possible right now!" I snapped impatiently as I ran upstairs to wake the same little girls that I had just forced to go to sleep. Tears dropped from my eyes as I literally stepped over my son four times to get his little sisters loaded into the car. He looked pitiful lying on the cold, ceramic floor holding the blood soaked compress to his chin.

I cried because I knew I was letting my son down by refusing to nurture him through his injury. I cried because I knew I wasn't going to get a break from the girls after all. I cried because the thought of babysitting two tired two-year-olds at the hospital while my four-year-old son got stitches was almost more than I could bear. I cried because I knew our day was going to be miserable. I cried because I knew none of my tears were for Gabriel, and I was so ashamed of feeling that way. The tears I cried were all for me; they were hopeless tears of self-pity.

Gabe ended up with seven stitches that day. During the appointment, the girls were thrilled to discover a whole box of heart monitor stickers. They delightfully decorated the entire room with their sticky treasures, much to the nurse's dismay. But honestly, what did she expect when she asked me to use both of my hands to hold Gabe's numbing medication on his chin for ten minutes? Hello? Did she not see the 2 two-year-olds in footed pajamas at my side? Ordinarily I would have never let them waste the hospital's supplies like they did. If she would have been willing to be the nurse, then I would have been free to be the mom. Since she didn't feel like doing her job, I wasn't going to stress myself out doing mine.

While it was just as frustrating of a visit as I had built up in my mind, ultimately we survived. Just like any other day, we made it through the chaos. However, I can guarantee you one thing: Gabe and I never again raced during naptime.

Unfortunately, though, there were some tasks that were unavoidable. I knew better than to attempt to take the kids shoe shopping unless I had adult help. But even this strategy failed to be foolproof during one horrendous shopping trip.

After the girls turned two, I recruited both my mom and Craig to help shop for new fall shoes and boots for the kids. Unfortunately, I woke up with a terrible head cold on the day we were supposed to go. I felt horrible. My head was foggy, my whole body was achy, and all I wanted to do was lay in bed. This was not a realistic option since I had three toddlers to take care of, so I decided to tough it out and move forward with the planned shoe trip. There was no way I was going to forfeit all the help that Craig and Mom would offer simply because of a cold.

When we got to the mall, my mom immediately parted to make a return so her hands would be free to help with the girls. Craig and I headed upstairs with the kids as my cold symptoms started to worsen. As we neared Nordstrom's shoe department, I leaned over on the double stroller and rested. I was short of breath and having a very hard time focusing due to the congestion in my head. When Craig announced he was going to the bathroom, I looked up just long enough to give him a dirty look. Of course he was going to the bathroom. Of course he was going to find any way that he could to get out of the madness that was to come. He'd been shoe shopping with us before. He knew what to expect.

Annoyed with Craig already, I asked Gabriel if he needed to go potty with Daddy. I was hoping his answer would be yes so that Craig would

143

have to take him with him. The last thing I needed was to be outnumbered 3-to-1 by my kids while I was trying to size the girls' feet. This was why I brought along adult help in the first place. What a lot of good that was.

When Gabe told me he didn't have to go, I begrudgingly took him to sit at the kids' table that Nordstrom provided for waiting children. They had a Thomas the Tank Engine track for the kids to play with, as well as *Finding Nemo* on TV. Since Gabriel was obsessed with both Thomas and Nemo, I assumed this would be a safe way to occupy him while I started browsing with the girls. I told him he was not to get up from the Thomas table without asking me first, and he agreed.

While the girls' love for shoes was useful during discipline, it was a nightmare in the middle of a children's shoe store. We knew better than to let them out of their side-by-side umbrella stroller. Experience had taught us that they would have picked up and tried on every shoe in sight, throwing them on the floor at the discovery of the next pair that caught their eyes. At least in their stroller they could only reach what was within arm's length, and it kept the inevitable shoe hurricane at a more reasonable level. Of course, they whined and cried to be set free from their stroller the entire time they were strapped in, which resulted in other patrons quietly disapproving of our loud and ill-behaved children.

As that day's luck would have it, a clerk waited on me almost immediately – before either Craig or my mom was there to help. Sizing the girls' feet was not a simple task. If Taylor got to go first, Sydney cried. If Sydney got to go first, Taylor cried. My attention soon became focused on keeping the peace between the girls as well as I could, all the while

144

making sure they were sized correctly so that I didn't have to repeat this dreaded process until absolutely necessary.

In the midst of refereeing my two crabby daughters, while the clerk was hunting for the shoes I requested in their sizes, I glanced up to check on Gabriel at the kids' table. Much to my surprise, he was not there. I did a quick scan of the entire shoe department. He was nowhere to be found.

"Gabriel?" I said in a loud voice, trying to sound calm as I turned in circles hunting for a glimpse of him.

Nothing.

"Gabe???" I yelled a bit louder, frustrated that I couldn't look as quickly as I wanted to because I had to maneuver the double-wide twin stroller through spaces that were entirely too narrow. He did not respond, and I still could not spot him.

"GABRIEL!!!!" I screamed, completely panicked this time.

"Ma'am, can I help you?" A Nordstrom employee noticed the uproar I was causing and came to assist me.

"I can't find my son!!" I shrieked.

Just then, I spotted Craig sauntering back towards the shoe department without a care in the world.

"CRAIG! Do you have Gabe???" I yelled, even though I could already see that he didn't have him.

"No! I don't have him! Where is he??" he asked, instantly joining me in my panic.

"I don't know! LOOK FOR HIM!" I yelled.

I felt so helpless! I couldn't leave the girls to look for Gabe, but the terror of not knowing if he was safe was crippling. I pushed the girls as fast as I could to the checkout counter and yelled to anyone who would listen, "Please, help! I can't find my son!"

Just then I heard a voice on the loudspeaker, "ATTENTION: ALL NORDSTROM EMPLOYEES. WE HAVE A CODE ADAM. I REPEAT: A CODE ADAM IS IN EFFECT. PLEASE FOLLOW STORE PROCEDURE AND LOCK DOWN ALL ENTRANCES AND EXITS."

Listening to this announcement, I was faced with my worst fear. I suddenly noticed the immediate adjacency of the kids' table to the large set of exit doors that led straight to the parking lot. My stomach flipped, and I felt the urge to vomit. "Oh my God, it's a kidnapper's dream," I thought to myself as my eyes began to fill. Gabriel could have been snatched out of the building and in a getaway car in less than five seconds. Terror-filled tears began to stream down my face.

"Ma'am, what does your son look like and what was he wearing?" the salesperson asked me in a sickeningly calm voice. My thoughts were everywhere. As I tried to remember what Gabriel was wearing, the trauma of the situation was making it next to impossible for me to focus.

"His name is Gabriel. He's only four! He has blonde hair and was wearing a blue and red striped shirt with jeans. Please find him!" I heard myself beg.

The lady picked up the phone and announced over the loudspeaker, "Attention:
The little boy is four years old. He has blonde hair and was wearing blue jeans with a red and blue striped shirt."

When she hung up the phone after making the announcement, I berated her. "That's it??? That's all you're going to do???"

"I'm sorry, but that's all we can do, Ma'am," she informed me apologetically. She instructed me to wait at the counter for further information.

"Kristin! What's wrong?!" I heard my mom yell as she rushed to the counter. She had heard the Code Adam description over the loudspeaker and had a sick feeling that the lost boy was her precious grandson. She was right.

"We can't find Gabriel! I don't know where he is!" I cried to her. She looked at me stunned, and started scanning Nordstrom frantically.

Thirty seconds later, which seemed like thirty minutes, the phone rang. The clerk answered on the first ring, listened briefly and then said, "Okay, thank you."
She hung up the phone, and then said with caution, "Ma'am, one of our employees thinks she has your little boy in the Junior department. She will keep him there until you arrive."

The Junior department?? That was on the other side of the store! I sprinted as fast as I could across the entirety of the third floor of Nordstrom. As I approached the Junior department, there was my sweet little boy holding on to the hand of a young brunette salesgirl.

"Oh, thank you!!!" I cried to her as I scooped him up in my arms.

Then I firmly stood him on the ground, grabbed both of his shoulders and looked him square in the eye. "Gabriel, what are you doing over here?? I told you NOT to leave the train table!"

As tears filled his eyes, he told the truth, "I had to go potty with Daddy, but I couldn't find him!"

I hugged him as hard as I could and we both cried together. "Sweetie, you can never go anywhere by yourself! We thought we lost you! We thought someone had taken you away from us! Don't *ever* do that again, okay?" I begged him.

"Okay, Mommy. I won't!" he promised.

It was one of the scariest moments of parenting I've ever experienced. I was emotionally exhausted. All I wanted to do was go home; but we still had to fit two temperamental twins with shoes. The only thing that mattered to them was that they had been torn away from the sparkly shoes they were about to try on.

What had happened was no one's fault. Gabe had changed his mind about going potty, and he thought he could catch up to his dad. Craig didn't know Gabe was following him so he took a shortcut amongst the clothing racks, which caused his four-year-old to lose sight of him. My typical two-year-old girls were distracting me, and my mom hadn't arrived to help yet.

Nonetheless, I should have known better than to place that much trust in a four-year-old little boy, even if he was the best behaved four-year-old I knew. I felt horrible for letting Gabe down. Losing him on that day felt like a metaphor for his daily existence. As usual, he had no choice but to suffer the ill consequences which accompanied the chaos of raising twins. He was such a good little boy, and it seemed so unfair that he was getting lost in the shuffle. I was disappointed in myself for failing my son. I loved those two little girls so much, but the amount of attention they required was draining. At two times two they seemed all powerful. There was nothing I could do to tame the little beasts.

148

Chapter 19: Coincidence?

Craig and I were very thankful for my mom's willingness to help with the kids. She would drive three hours from Cleveland whenever we asked her for the help and support that we needed. Honestly speaking, she would drive three hours from Cleveland even when we *didn't* ask her to come. Before the girls were born, Gabriel was her first and only grandchild. He grew so accustomed to hearing me tell Craig "My mom is coming" that Gabe naturally assumed "My mom" was her name. As a result, he took to calling her "Memom." She treasured the nickname, and it became her favorite term of endearment.

Memom adored her grandbabies, and needless to say her love was more than reciprocated. They would jump for joy when she arrived, and cry at the window as they watched her car drive away. As much work as they were, Memom never minded the chaos. She would willingly babysit all three kids whenever Craig and I felt as though we needed a break. Sometimes, when she could tell my nerves were getting really fried, she would insist that I leave them with her so that I could have some time to myself to rejuvenate. Whether she watched them at our house or hers, she volunteered to do the driving to keep things as simple as possible for Craig and me. She generously sacrificed her time, which is the greatest gift a mother can give.

Leaving them with my mom was always easy. Because she visited so frequently, she knew the ins and outs of our daily routine. She knew all the different ways to pacify each of the kids when they were upset. She knew what foods they liked and what foods to avoid. She was very much in tune with the current phases of each child at any given stage of development. In some ways she probably knew more about the kids' needs than even Craig, and he was more than happy to pass the torch when she was around. He was never too proud to admit that he appreciated the breaks from parenthood she afforded him. Because he knew it made her so happy to be that involved, it really was a win-win for both of them.

As a result of this relationship, Craig and I fully trusted her to take perfect care of them when we were gone. After all, her favorite pastime was granting them her undivided attention. She had mastered the art of spoiling them without forgetting to provide structure and discipline when necessary, which was very important to us. She was their favorite babysitter, which allowed us to leave without any cause for concern.

We were more than thrilled when my mom and her husband, Grandpa Bob, agreed to buy a summer lake house thirty minutes north of us after the girls were born. We welcomed their company, and knew we would benefit greatly from steady seasonal help with the kids. On one such evening that Memom was babysitting at the lake house, Craig and I returned home from a fun and relaxing date-night spent without our pest, Chaos. Gabriel was four and the girls were still terribly two.

As usual, when I walked in the house I asked, "How did they do, Memom?"

"Well...they did okay," she hesitated.

"Uh-oh," I reacted. I could tell there was more to the story, and it wasn't going to be good. "What happened?" I asked, prepared for tales of disobedience or mass destruction.

"Well, the girls went upstairs and got really quiet. So I went to find out what they were up to," she explained. She was referring to the general rule of thumb that if we could hear them, they were okay; but when the girls got quiet, it was a sure sign they were up to no good.

"When I walked into my bedroom, I found Sydney with this," she frowned as she produced an empty bottle of Children's Tylenol Cold Medicine.

"Uh-oh," I repeated. "Was it empty before she got hold of it?"

"Well, not exactly," she cushioned her words. "There was this much left," she explained while using her thumb and index finger to measure approximately 1 ½ inches worth of medicine. This dangerous piece of news caused my eyes to grow large with concern.

"You think she drank it all?" I asked, needing her to clarify.

"I wish I knew," she admitted honestly. "There was some medicine running down her chin and onto her belly when I found her. So she obviously spilled some. I can't say for sure how much she really swallowed," she said as she scrunched up her face apologetically.

"When did she drink it?" I asked, trying to find all the pieces to the puzzle.

"About fifteen minutes ago," she said as she looked at her watch. "I knew you were on your way so I figured I'd wait to see how you wanted to handle it."

"Did you call Poison Control?" I asked.

"No, but I've been watching her closely and there doesn't appear to be anything wrong with her," she assessed optimistically.

151

"Craig, get me the phone and find the number for Poison Control," I directed him. While he dialed Poison Control, I continued to interrogate my mom. I needed every detail available so I could accurately relay the situation to the poison specialist.

"Mom," I asked as Craig handed me the phone, "are you sure it was only Sydney who drank the syrup?"

"Yes," she declared. "I know it was Sydney. She was holding the bottle when I walked in, and Taylor didn't have a drop on her. I honestly don't think Taylor could have gotten it to her mouth without spilling some on herself," she explained her theory.

I was satisfied with this answer. Taylor struggled to eat or drink anything without spilling it all over the floor or herself. She was an extremely messy little girl.

I soon learned from the girl at Poison Control that Sydney had ingested what could be a dangerous amount of cold medicine. She recommended that we take her to the emergency room to be evaluated by a doctor. Five minutes later, Mom and I were in the car with Sydney en-route to the hospital. Craig and Grandpa stayed behind with Taylor and Gabriel.

I called Craig when we got there to double check on Taylor. I wanted to be sure that she hadn't ingested any of the medicine without us being aware of it. He told me that she was perfectly fine. She was full of energy and almost impossible to tame, as usual.

It was becoming more and more obvious that Mom was right and Sydney had, indeed, been the one who overdosed on the medicine. Not only did her heart monitors prove that she had an accelerated heartbeat, but she was also extremely groggy. The doctor didn't feel comfortable sending her home until she had been monitored for at least two hours.

I called Craig to update him, and again I inquired about Taylor's state of health. Once again, he reassured me she was just fine. He told me to kiss Sydney and send her his love, and then we hung up. I put my phone back in my purse and switched it to vibrate so that the ringer wouldn't disturb Sydney and the other patients. I snuggled on the gurney with my sweet little girl and prayed for the best.

Two hours later, the doctor sent us home. Her heartbeat was back to a normal pace, and he felt it was safe to release her. We were instructed to watch her very closely and wake her up every two hours to ensure she was conscious and alert. If she vomited we were to take her to the hospital immediately. This would have been a sign that the poison was continuing to take a toll on her body.

I was relieved Sydney had been discharged, but still a bit uneasy about the questionable nature of her health. I decided to sleep beside her that night in order to keep a safe watch over her. I pulled my phone from my purse to call Craig to tell him we were heading home. When I looked down to dial, I was shocked to discover that I had missed thirteen calls from him.

"Mom! Craig called thirteen times!" I exclaimed, confused and panicked.

"What?" she asked. "When???" she demanded.

"While we were in the room! My phone was on vibrate, so I didn't hear it ring!" I explained to her. I quickly dialed Craig's number.

"Kristin!" he answered, or rather yelled.

"What is going on?" I demanded to know.

"Why didn't you answer your phone??" he hissed at me, completely frustrated.

"I'm sorry! I didn't hear it!" I said, annoyed that he was dwelling on the unimportant details. "Forget about the phone!" I commanded. "What's going on??"

"I don't *know* what's going on!" he said, annoyed in return, "Taylor has puked three times!" This development startled me as the doctor had just warned me that vomiting was a dangerous symptom.

"Mom!" I said. "Are you absolutely *positive* that Taylor didn't drink the medicine?" I begged her for clarity. "Taylor has thrown up three times!"

"Kristin," she declared, "I am almost 100% sure that she didn't drink any. If they both drank it, there wouldn't have been enough in the bottle for them to share and have it still be a dangerous amount," she reasoned.

I hung up with Craig and tracked down the ER doctor that had just dismissed us. After I explained the situation, he left it up to me as to whether or not I wanted to bring Taylor in to repeat the monitoring process we'd just endured with Sydney. We agreed that I would decide once I had a chance to evaluate Taylor's behavior myself.

When we arrived home at eleven o'clock, Taylor was buzzing around the house without a care in the world. Craig had kept her up intentionally, well aware of the fact that I would need to assess her with my own eyes. Sydney was still very drowsy from the medicine, and wanted nothing to do with her hyper sister. The dramatic difference in energy levels made it obvious to me that Taylor had not ingested too much medicine, if any. Her

154

eyes were clear and alert. She was active and completely herself, which was in direct contrast to her groggy, foggy-eyed sister.

Still puzzled, I asked Craig to describe the "puke." He told me that on three different occasions she paused her play, walked over to him with her arms outstretched in need of comforting, and then proceeded to spit up a bile-like substance. He admitted that technically it wasn't vomit and the description of her "puking" was, perhaps, a bit overdramatic.

"It was gross, I was worried, and you wouldn't pick up your phone!" he interrupted and self-excused when I began to lecture him about the importance of accurate details. I ended up dropping the lecture, as I already knew three facts:

1: Craig is horrible in case of an emergency. He goes straight to panic mode.

2: Craig is repulsed by vomit. The fact that he had to clean spit-up three times was enough to put him over the edge.

3: I knew he was mad that I didn't think to check my phone while his daughter was in the hospital, and I couldn't blame him for feeling that way.

Ultimately, we decided that Taylor was acting too normal to merit a trip to the ER. We tucked them both into the queen bed that I would be sharing with them and hoped for the best. Both girls responded as they were supposed to when I woke them up throughout the night, and were back to their normal selves the following day.

Our experience from the previous night provided interesting conversation over coffee the next morning. We had heard strange tales of medical coincidences occurring between sets of twins, and we all agreed that the girls had experienced their first true "twin-moment." While Sydney was in distress at the hospital, Taylor was exhibiting symptoms on her sister's behalf. There just didn't seem to be any other explanation.

As we were learning, lots of things concerning the twins defied normal logic. Atypical was typical...twin-style. Unfortunately this wouldn't be the last time we found ourselves at the doctor's trying to solve medical mysteries provided by our twin daughters.

Chapter 20: Survival of the Fittest

As I've mentioned before, Sydney and Taylor were premature babies. Because of this, they both struggled to overcome developmental obstacles. Whether it was rolling over, sitting, crawling, walking or talking, the girls had to work harder than most babies to conquer these tasks. Because these are the developmental milestones that occur in plain sight, it was readily apparent the girls had problems which needed to be addressed. Occupational Therapy was required for their low muscle-tone and lack of coordination, and Speech Therapy was a necessity to help them learn to talk. While both practices were expensive, time-consuming and painstakingly slow remedies, consistent and steady evidence of forward progress reassured us that we were on the right track to helping them achieve a "normal" state of being.

This is the black and white version of the story. These are the facts afforded to us with hindsight. While we were living through the constant worry and uncertainty of our daughters' physical and cognitive potential, life for all of us felt like a never-ending, emotional roller coaster ride.

While both girls struggled, especially with their speech, we worried the most about Sydney. She was forever lagging behind her twin sister. In fact, learning how to talk almost killed Sydney.

After thorough evaluations, both girls were diagnosed with severe Apraxia of Speech. This condition is a motor-speech programming disorder resulting in the inability to voluntarily produce sounds, words, phrases and sentences. The girls could hear and understand the words of others, but they couldn't change what they heard into the fine-motor skill of combining consonants and vowels to form their own words. They could take language in, but could not spit language out. As a result, at the age of two they both spent two hours per week in intense Speech and Occupational Therapy. The Occupational Therapy would also benefit their speech as they focused on sensory integration and oral-motor skills.

While they were drilled over and over again during speech, the girls would learn how to break language down to its simplest form in order to begin to overcome their handicaps. Their progress was *slow*. It took six months for them to finally start saying words and short phrases on their own.

Taylor seemed to handle the therapy very well. The only issue that had to be addressed with her was her lack of focus, which led to ill behavior. At $50 per half hour, she didn't have time to be naughty. When she did focus, though, it was encouraging to watch her through the observation window because I could tell she was getting it. She could do what her teacher asked her to do, and it didn't appear to be exceedingly difficult for her. I could tell that even though it would take a million little baby steps, in due time Taylor would learn to leap on her own.

However, speech therapy was painful for Sydney. As I sympathetically watched her during her lessons, her state of overwhelming discomfort was obvious. The amount of focus and concentration it required for her to produce the most basic of sounds was almost unfathomable. The process was exhausting for her. During her half hour, she yawned incessantly, and rubbed her face over and over again as though she was trying to stay awake. She tugged on her hair in frustration, and squirmed in her seat with unsettling distress when asked to produce specific sounds or words. She was miserable during speech, but there was no way we could pull her out

158

of it. At two and a half, she had to push through the discomfort of learning to talk.

I worried about Sydney all the time. I was concerned that she was perhaps autistic. So many things seemed to be "off" with her personality. We were having a horrible time with her at home, and we were scared something was really wrong. This was not because she was misbehaving, but rather because she was losing consciousness on a regular basis.

As I said before, Sydney did everything after Taylor. Not just the basic things (like rolling, sitting, crawling and walking,) but other abstract things as well. For example, a few months earlier, Taylor had thrown one of her famous temper tantrums. In the midst of her raging fit, she did not gasp for air as children do after they've started the initial wail. Instead, she turned blue, her extremities stiffened, her eyes rolled to the back of her head, and she passed out. Assuming she was having a seizure, we were scared to death! As I blew a big breath of air into her limp little mouth, Craig sprinted to the phone to call 9-1-1. Immediately, though, she started to breathe again. Then she cried in fear of what had just happened to her. Once I comforted her and reassured her that she was okay, she was perfectly normal.

Freaked out of my mind, I called our pediatrician and explained to her what had just occurred. She told me it sounded as if Taylor had experienced a "breath-holding spell." This meant that she had intentionally not taken a breath because she was so angry: the Mother of all temper tantrums. She dramatically opted not to breathe. Most of the time, when breath-holders pass out they will immediately regain consciousness on their own. If it were to happen again, she instructed me to ignore her over the

159

top attention-getting device, and just make sure that CPR wasn't necessary. I couldn't believe it. I had never heard anything like it before!

Thankfully, Taylor only had one more breath-holding spell. I was home alone and I did exactly what the doctor told me to do, even though internally I was panicked. She lost consciousness in the middle of the floor where she was throwing her fit. I watched her out of the corner of my eye to make sure CPR wasn't necessary. Just as the doctor predicted, she regained consciousness on her own immediately thereafter. When she came back from her self-induced spell, I ignored her request to be comforted. Instead of coddling her, I told her she was a bad girl and walked away from her. My reaction made her furious, but she never held her breath again.

Two weeks later, Sydney got angry enough to execute her first breath-holding spell. But because I was familiar with this form of temper tantrum from my experience with Taylor, I was only annoyed by Sydney's imitation of her sister's naughty behavior

As if praying for breath during these temper tantrums wasn't enough, one Sunday we were served with an even scarier set of circumstances. We were having an enjoyable evening as a family for a change. The mood was actually low key, quiet, and peaceful. Gabriel was watching *Toy Story* in the playroom, and the girls were in the family room with us. They were contentedly coloring at their play-table and babbling in their twin-talk. Craig and I were liberated as we relaxed on the couch, basking in the unexpected simplicity of the evening. It was so refreshing to regard our girls with adoration, instead of frustration.

160

In a split second, our evening abruptly changed from quiet contentment to panicked chaos. The girls had been snacking on clementine slices when, all of a sudden, Taylor stood and ran to me with a look of horror in her eyes. Her face was beat red, and she was eerily silent.

"Oh my God, Craig! She's choking!" I exclaimed as I sprang towards her.

I picked her up and performed the Heimlich maneuver over and over again, but I could not dislodge the piece of fruit that was blocking her airway. I did a finger-swipe of her mouth, but found nothing. I tipped her upside down and beat her back in an upward motion with the heel of my hand. When she still could not utter a sound, panic consumed me.

"Craig! I can't get it out!!!!" I screamed. "CALL 9-1-1!"

As Craig ran for the phone, Taylor's face turned a lifeless shade of blue, her little hands sickled, and her eyes rolled into the back of her head as she passed out. She looked exactly as if she were having a breath-holding spell, only this time I knew for a fact that it was not voluntary. If I didn't figure out how to help her quickly, my sweet baby girl was going to die in my arms in a matter of seconds.

"Don't you die, Taylor! You cannot die, Taylor!" I willed her to live.

I felt completely helpless. Even though I knew I wasn't supposed to according to medical choking standards, I crammed my finger down her throat in a desperate attempt to find the Clementine. Luckily, I caught it with my fingertip and carefully scraped it up and out of her throat. By now, she was already unconscious and not breathing. I quickly tilted her head back and pinched the top of her nose to open her airway. I prayed as I placed my mouth over hers to offer her one long breath of air and all the love I

161

could muster. Her little eyes popped open, full of terror. We were both shaking from fear, but at least she was alive. We clutched each other tightly and cried together as the intensity of the situation registered with both of us.

When the ambulance arrived a couple of minutes later, she had already settled back down. To be sure she was okay, the paramedics checked her thoroughly. Just the presence of the rescue team in our house was a haunting reminder as to how close we came to losing our little girl. After they left, we all sat in silence. We were humbled to have made it through with a positive outcome. We had to fight back the nauseating question of "What if?" because to consider the alternative was more than we could bear to imagine.

Three months later, Sydney choked on a piece of muskmelon. After several failed Heimlich maneuvers, she too lost consciousness. I again retrieved the foreign object with my finger, gave her a breath of air and brought her back to life. The same panic filled our house. The same intensity nearly suffocated us. The same haunting question of "What if?" was terrifying. However, different from Taylor, this would not be the last time that Sydney would choke so severely that she would lose consciousness.

While Taylor had given up her breath-holding spells long ago, Sydney was having them regularly. What was worse was that when she passed out her body would go so limp that she would urinate. The scariest part about Sydney's breath-holding spells was that it didn't appear as if they were intentional. Sometimes it happened when she wasn't even mad, but rather after she had fallen and hurt herself. Because these incidents weren't always the results of tantrums, I was perplexed as to why she was having so many of them. I couldn't help but wonder if she simply didn't have enough

162

command over the muscles in her body to be able to resist the outward flow of air in order to inhale. It seemed as if she was losing consciousness at least once every two weeks.

Even more concerning was that Sydney also continued to choke in a life-threatening manner. The second time she choked was on a peanut M&M. Again, it was as if someone had lied about this damn Heimlich maneuver thing, because it *never* worked! I knew for a fact I was doing it correctly! I had made sure of that by having my pediatrician practice with me at our last appointment.

She urinated on herself as she lost consciousness. I was dialing 9-1-1 as she lost all function of her body. Before I could press the final digit, the peanut M&M dislodged and she resumed breathing.

So now I noticed a pattern: It was only when Sydney lost consciousness that her little body would release the foreign objects. I made an immediate appointment with her pediatrician to discuss the situation, because I absolutely could not live with the constant fear of Sydney choking on food anymore. I was referred to an Ear, Nose and Throat specialist who suggested the removal of her tonsils and adenoids. They were enlarged, which could possibly be the reason the lodged food couldn't eject out of her esophagus when given the Heimlich. While this made good sense, there was an internal voice in me that questioned the validity of the diagnosis. I was hesitant to jump on board and make the appointment, but I didn't know what else to do. I was willing to try anything to save my daughter's life, so I went ahead and scheduled the surgery.

She was to have her tonsils and adenoids out the following month. At this point I was terrified to leave the girls with anyone. We were plagued with anxiety during every breakfast, lunch, dinner, and snack time. It was impossible to enjoy a meal. We cut the girls' food into miniscule size bites so small that my one-year-old niece, Lauren, who only had four teeth, was eating larger pieces of food than the twins.

If we had to leave the girls with a babysitter, I refused to leave until I could feed them myself. I left strict instructions for the babysitter as to what they could have for a snack, and it was always something choke-free like yogurt. I warned the sitters to the point of scaring them that Sydney had a strong tendency to choke. Both of my babysitters knew that if there was any suspicion one of the girls may be choking, they were to immediately, with no hesitations, call 9-1-1. Even if it turned out to be a false alarm, I wanted the paramedics on alert.

I was a nervous wreck, and rightfully so. Sydney choked for the third major time while eating a snack of dry Cheerios. Due to the fact that Cheerios have holes in the middle of them and dissolve almost instantly, they are said to be choke-proof. Some even consider it safe to let a six-month-old baby snack on Cheerios. Sydney would beg to differ.

Confident they were both snacking calmly, I made a quick run upstairs to grab the pile of dirty clothes I had previously gathered before snack time. Because they were eating, I immediately came back downstairs to the kitchen. More out of habit and paranoia than true concern, I needed to check on the girls' safety. After all, they were eating Cheerios. What could go wrong with Cheerios?

As I entered the kitchen, I saw Sydney struggling to get out of her chair. This was a sign of imminent danger I had come to recognize all too well. Her face was plastered with desperate fear because she could not breathe.

She was trying to get to me so I would save her life. I sprinted toward her. I spun her around immediately and performed the Heimlich. I repeatedly lifted and squeezed her so hard that it felt as though I would break her, to no avail. I turned her upside down and struck her back with such force that I thought I might leave a bruise. Still nothing. As she started to turn blue, I searched her throat with my finger. I couldn't find the blockage. However, I was running out of time quickly. Before I could pull my finger out of her mouth, Sydney's jaw clenched as her body stiffened before she lost consciousness. My finger was stuck; locked between her razor-sharp baby teeth. Pain and panic were piercing through me as I realized, "Oh my God. This might be it. This might be the time that I can't save her."

With Sydney in my arms, I raced to the phone in the laundry room for help. As I rounded the corner out of the kitchen, I slipped on Gabriel's favorite knitted blanket that was lying on the floor. My feet flew out from under me, and I was airborne. My body flew through the air horizontally with my choking toddler still in my arms. As my body came crashing down, my head banged on the ceramic floor. No longer able to hold on to her, Sydney flew out of my arms and crashed to the floor three feet away from me. I saw her little head hit the floor as well, and I was terrified. Before I could get to her though, I miraculously heard her gasp for air, and a soft moan escaped her throat. With God's hand to keep her safe, the jolt of the fall was enough to jar the blockage out of her airway.

I grabbed her and held her tight against my chest as she regained consciousness. As she opened her horror-filled eyes, she clutched my neck. My heart was pounding with such intensity I felt as though I might pass out too. My brain was straining to process the enormity of the situation, but

165

shock was keeping me from making any sense of it. What possessed me to run to the laundry room in the first place? There wasn't even a phone in there. We had moved the cordless base that had previously been in the laundry room into the kitchen more than a month ago!

Still confused and shaken, I started to feel wet heat on my legs. I looked down to discover Sydney had peed all over me and the blue blanket I just slipped on. I reached for the blanket to get it out from underneath me so that we weren't sitting in a pool of urine. But when she saw the blanket, she reached for it for comfort. It was soaked with pee, and I didn't want her nuzzling it to her face like she always did when she was upset.

"Honey, this blankie has pee-pee all over it and it's yucky," I tried to explain to her. She didn't care. She still wanted the disgusting blanket.

"Mommy will go get you a new blankie, honey," I tried to reason with her.

"No!" she argued with me, as she pointed at the urine-sopped blanket that I was still holding in my hand. I realized the only way I could distract her from wanting this blanket was if I made it disappear entirely. I temporarily sat her down on the floor and opened the door to the garage. I hid the wet blanket behind my back as I backed down the two steps to the garage while maintaining eye contact with her the entire time. She was still crying, but no longer hysterical. She was distracted by the blanket and was curious to see what I was going to do with it. I quickly tossed the blanket to the side, where it was no longer visible to her. I planned to pick her back up and take her to find her favorite yellow and blue blankie instead. However, as I started to go back into the house, suddenly Taylor appeared in the doorway with a devilish grin. Before I knew what was happening,

166

the large wooden door promptly slammed shut in my face. Taylor was initiating a game, completely oblivious to what was going on. I reached to open the door so that I could reconnect with Sydney, knowing she was still upset. But before I had a chance to twist the knob, I heard a loud CLICK.

My other two-year-old had just dead-bolted me out of my house.

"Taylor, unlock the door!" I shouted. What was I saying? She didn't even know she had locked it; much less know how to unlock it. She was imitating what she saw me do every time I closed the door when we were home alone.

"Taylor, turn the knob on the top again, sweetie! Please, honey, listen to Mommy!" I begged and prayed at the same time.

I heard her fiddling with the deadbolt in an attempt to follow my instructions, but she couldn't figure out how to turn it back to its vertical, unlocked position. She could barely reach it in the first place. What were the odds that she was going to understand that she had to turn it back in the opposite direction?

I could hear Sydney begin to cry again. Not only had I taken away her comfort object, but now I had deserted her too.

"Sydney! Just a second, honey! Mommy can't open the door!" I tried to calm her, but I was getting nowhere. A wave of nauseated frenzy consumed me as I suddenly realized there was no reason for any other doors to the house to be unlocked. This was the only door that had yet been used that day when Craig and Gabe left through the garage to go to work and school. Taylor had just locked it in my face! My cell phone was also in the house with my two-year-old twins, one of whom had nearly choked to death only seconds before!

"Girls, please listen to Mommy!" I begged them for their attention.

I could hear Taylor happily babbling back at me on the other side of the door, while Sydney was still sobbing.

"Mommy has to go find help because I can't get the door open. But I need you to stay *right there!* Do *not* move! Mommy will be right back!" I promised them, hoping it was true. I was sick to my stomach out of concern for their safety. I knew that it was just plain dangerous to leave 2 two-year-olds unattended in the house for even the shortest amount of time.

Still in my pajamas, I sprinted outside trying to decide what to do. I noticed a landscaper across the street, and I cringed at thought of having to tell him why I needed to use his phone. My greater fear was if he didn't have a phone, I was going to have to resort to knocking on my neighbors' door in order to ask for help. If I thought they had talked about us before, my God, what would they say now?

With this in mind, I had to at least rule out the possibility that no other doors to the house were unlocked. I ran up the sidewalk to the front door, but just as I had suspected, it was locked. It had been raining for days, and as I ran barefoot around the side of the house I sank to my ankles in mud. I only had two chances left as I made my way to the back of the house. I went first to the door that would most likely be open: no luck. As I approached the final door, I was hopeless. Of all the doors on our house, we used this one the very least, so the chances of it being unlocked were slim to none.

"Please, God...let this door be open!" I prayed from the bottom of my heart. I closed my eyes tightly as I attempted to turn the knob, willing the door handle to turn freely. I was shocked when I felt the handle continue to move downward as the door-latch popped open. By the grace of God, the door was unlocked. This was the second miracle of the day.

"Girls!" I yelled, trying to swallow the enormous lump of gratitude swelling in my throat. "Mommy is downstairs!!"

"Yaaayyy!! Momma!!!!" I heard Taylor shout with approval of this fantastically fun game.

I ran upstairs as fast as my muddy feet would allow. Sydney was still sniffling as she reached for me, and I hugged her as tightly as I could.

"Oh, sissy! I am so sorry!" I apologized to her profusely. "Let's go get your blankie!" I bargained with her. Sydney smiled and shook her head in agreement. She was already done being mad at me. Taylor trotted along happily behind us, never knowing there was a problem in the first place.

As I grabbed Sydney's yellow and blue blankie, I glanced at the clock.

"Oh my gosh, girls!" I exclaimed, stunned. "We've got to go pick up Gabe *right now!*" Instinctively, I was still desperate to cuddle Sydney, but reality only allowed me ten minutes to get to Gabe's pre-school for dismissal. The trip alone took twelve minutes, and I still had to change Sydney's wet clothes and get the girls loaded into the car. I had no choice but to continue to bottle my emotions in order to take care of the needs of all three of my children.

I was fifteen minutes late to pick up Gabriel that day, and when I picked him up, I was still in my pajamas. My life was spiraling out of control. My daughter had nearly choked to death before my very eyes. My other daughter locked me out of the house, causing another whole set of worries and dangers to present themselves. All the while, my little boy was wondering why his mommy wasn't there to pick him up from school.

169

On our way home, my brother called to ask when we were planning to arrive on our next visit. Considering my emotional state at the time, I couldn't for the life of me discuss mundane plans concerning the future. Hell, I was going to be lucky to just to make it through the day. When I told him I didn't know the answer, I could tell by his response he was frustrated. That was all it took.

"*Dusty*! You have *no* idea what I've been through today! I've had the worst day of my life! Sydney almost choked to death until I dropped her on her head, Taylor locked me out of the house before I could make sure Sydney was okay, and I just picked up Gabe late in my pajamas!" I sobbed all of this hysterically into the phone. I was crying so hard I could barely catch my breath.

"Okay...is everyone alright?" he asked, probably the most concerned for my sanity.

"Yes. We're fine! I just really can't talk about this right now!" I vented.

"Do you want me to call back later?" I could tell he was confused, but hopeful.

"*YES!*" I said as I slammed my flip-phone shut and threw it on the floor of the van.

I was mortified. My brother had already upgraded the title of our household from "The Show" to "The Zoo", which was more than annoying. He had no idea the challenges we faced on a daily basis. How could he? He was still floating through the simple life with only one child. Even though I remembered how much easier it was when we only had Gabe, all I could hear in his tone of voice was judgment - whether it existed or not. In my heart of hearts, I knew I was a good mom. Today, though, I was defeated.

170

While I thought I was crying because I assumed my brother was judging me, in reality I was the one judging myself.

I was drowning. I felt like giving up because the odds were stacked so high against me. Would Sydney *ever* stop choking? How were we going to keep the girls alive through the age of two? Would this phase *ever* end, or was this just my life from now on? If so, where in the world was I going to find the strength to endure?

I had heard that God never gave you more than you could handle, but I was starting to question this philosophy in a hurry. I loved the girls so much, but they wore me down to nothingness on a daily basis. Would I ever just get to *enjoy* my daughters? Or was their existence always going to be clouded by one fiasco after another?

Chapter 21: Ya Don't Say?

I distinctly remember Gabriel's two-year-old check up. His doctor told me that my most important job for the next year was to keep him from killing himself. I thought it was strange advice at the time, and I wondered if she was actually serious. When the girls were two, I really got it. Not only did I get it, but I also appreciated the fair warning. I knew that in order to keep Sydney alive I was going to need further professional assistance.

Every bit of maternal instinct I possessed was screaming for a concrete medical diagnosis to explain Sydney's frequent and life threatening choking episodes. After the Cheerio incident, I knew without a doubt that there was something more serious going on than just inadequate chewing on her part or enlarged tonsils. It was a fact that the only way her airway would clear was if she lost consciousness. Every time her body went limp and her muscles completely relaxed, she would start breathing again.

My theory was that she was having an esophageal spasm that wouldn't allow her food to pass down into her stomach or back up into her mouth. I called my favorite and most trusted pediatrician and made an appointment to discuss my hypothesis. She also found it to be curious that Sydney's loss of consciousness proved to be more helpful than detrimental. She referred us to a Pediatric Digestive Care Clinician who performed an endoscopy on Sydney's esophagus.

When the camera traveled down her throat and into her stomach, it revealed an ulcer located between the base of her esophagus and the top of her stomach lining. The ulcer was causing acid reflux. When she swallowed, her reflux would kick in. The acids from her stomach traveled up her esophagus as the food was traveling down, therefore creating a roadblock. When the food got stuck in her airway, the Heimlich maneuver was ineffective because her tonsils were so irritated and enlarged from the acid reflux. When she lost consciousness the reflux subsided, the acid receded, and her esophagus relaxed; thus, allowing the food to pass one way or another.

After six weeks on Prevacid Sydney was like a new child, and even started to experience some success at speech. She was finally able to produce the names of some objects on her own which caused her stress level to dissipate. She was actually starting to enjoy her lessons.

I believe the stress of speech therapy - her knowing the name of an object in her head but not being able to summon and produce the word - is what caused her to develop an ulcer. Once she finally figured out how to get her brain and her tongue to cooperate, with the help of the antacid prescription, her ulcer was able to heal. When the ulcer went away, her reflux subsided and her inflamed tonsils shrunk to a safer size. As a result, she eventually stopped choking. Still, leaving nothing to chance, we went ahead with her tonsillectomy as a precautionary measure.

Does this mean we pushed Sydney too hard in Speech Therapy? One could argue that, I suppose. On the other hand, she would have endured just as much stress if we enabled her to fail at speech while her identical twin learned to talk. Any parents of twins learn early, and are constantly reminded, that it's impossible to make a decision about the needs of one twin without considering the ramifications it will have on the other. Sydney needed to keep pace with her sister's ability to communicate so she didn't get left behind.

The girls' inability to express themselves often triggered their misbehavior and led to our collective family frustration. They couldn't tell us what they wanted and, therefore, would act out in defiance when we couldn't understand or fulfill their needs.

It's no different than the frustration I feel when I talk to my mom when her hearing aid batteries are low. I repeat myself over and over again, and ultimately end up losing my patience because I'm tired of speaking and not being heard. I realize it's not her fault, but nevertheless it's extremely frustrating, and I wonder if she's really paying attention to me in the first place.

This had to have been how the girls felt towards everyone the first few years of their lives. They would speak, and it seemed as if no one would listen to them. Meanwhile, we were listening as closely as we could, but were not able decipher what it was that they were trying to say.

Speech was helping our whole family heal. Little did we know that even though it would be a very long and tedious process, their ability to communicate was the most effective weapon we had to battle chaos. While we were noticing great results at home, it was still nearly impossible for anyone other than myself to understand what they were saying, which made public conversation stressfully unrealistic. I always encouraged them to answer for themselves, but inevitably I would need to provide a translation for their audience.

On the rare occasions people addressed the girls' speech delays with me in an upfront, honest and caring manner, I was more than willing to talk about their struggles. In fact, I liked to talk about the subject. We had nothing to hide and we were certainly not ashamed of them. It was good to vent every now and again, and it also allowed us to gain perspective from others who had helpful insight to share. We knew that it was a very real and serious obstacle to contend with, but we were on top of it. We just preferred that if people were curious about their speech they would respect us enough to ask us about it directly. There was no need to beat around the bush, because, quite frankly, it was insulting.

Unfortunately, no matter where we went, people who heard them talk would ask, "*How old* did you say they were?"

"Well, *actually*, I hadn't mentioned their ages yet..." I felt like retorting just to make them feel as stupid as they sounded. Did these people truly believe we couldn't hear the condescension in their voices? Did they expect us to think that they cared about their ages instead of their poor speech? Did they actually assume they were the first ones noticing the girls' obvious speech delays? Did they really believe it was possible that I spent all day every day with them, and wasn't aware of the fact that their communication skills were lacking?

I was constantly baffled by the insensitivity of grown adults. How could they be so rude and judgmental of two little girls standing right in front of them? I would have loved to point out the obvious, "They're two, and even though they don't talk very well, their ears work just fine. They can hear the negative intonation in your voice, and *by the way*...so can I."

Fortunately, I possessed a little more tact than they did. So instead, I would respond with a simple number depending on their age at the given time of questioning. That was it; I offered no justification for their speech. I played the idiot, pretending my feelings were not hurt by their insensitive remarks. Even though I was fully aware they were digging for an

175

explanation about the lack of clarity in their speech instead of their ages, I never wanted the girls to hear me make excuses for them. While I knew they had speech issues to contend with, I needed them to be confident in the fact that I loved them exactly the way they were. I had complete faith in their ability to overcome their Apraxia. Their poor speech did not define them, and I wasn't about to waste my time indulging in conversation with those who thought differently.

All I cared about was that my girls continued to make forward progress with their speech, which benefitted our whole family dynamic. As the girls began to speak in phrases, life got easier. Our frustration level declined as their linguistic abilities grew. They could tell us what they needed, and we could provide it for them. In turn, they no longer felt the need to act out in retribution.

Even though we still had a long way to go, we were beginning to tip the scales of balance. The prospect of being able to enjoy the company of our daughters no longer seemed improbable.

Chapter 22: Watch What You Wish For...

While Taylor and Sydney's improved speech had a positive effect on our entire household environment, there was no denying the fact we were in the throes of raising 2 two-year-olds. There were still moments when the complexity of their ages, behavior, and lack of development would cause us to stumble.

A visit to a restaurant could turn into a trip from hell. Drinks were forever being spilled, the floor often held more food than the children's stomachs, and the trips to the bathroom were never-ending as we were potty training 2 two-year-olds.

During one such trip to a restaurant, Taylor had thrown a beastly temper tantrum because I wouldn't let her go into the dirty bathroom stall by herself. To make her point, she slammed the door...right on her finger. After examining her purple finger to be sure it wasn't broken, I scolded her. She was appalled by my lack of sympathy. To get even, she screamed even louder. As we exited the bathroom, I was "that mom" as I drug Taylor back to the table by the crook of her elbow. She did her best to hang on to her temper tantrum for affect, our food took forever to arrive, someone burnt their mouth on a hot fry, and the lid of a kid's cup fell off and drenched a plateful of food with chocolate milk. All in all, nothing had gone right. My head was pounding from the ordeal. I ordered a glass of wine with dinner, which did nothing to ease the almost palpable tension.

When we finally made it back to the van, I wasn't in the mood to drive. I wanted to plop into the passenger seat and close my eyes. However, because the girls were used to being with me all the time, they preferred it when I drove. When Craig got behind the wheel, they cried and screamed in unison, "No, Momma di! Momma di!" ("Momma drive, Momma drive!") Usually when this happened, Craig and I would switch seats to satisfy them, because it didn't seem like a battle worth fighting.

On this particular evening though, I had no patience for their shenanigans. After feeling so out of control inside the restaurant, I was in the mood to win a battle for a change. So when the girls voiced their usual objections, I was having none of it. I turned around from the passenger seat to face them.

"Girls, I am NOT driving tonight!" I spit with venom.

As if on cue, they both burst into loud, dramatic wails.

"Momma di! Momma di!" They started in on their usual tirade.

"*Girls!*" I regained their attention. "Mommy *cannot* drive tonight. I had alcohol at dinner, and when you drink alcohol you *cannot* drive." I laid down the law.

Now, granted, it was impossible for them to understand the logic behind this statement, but apparently they sensed the seriousness with which the message was delivered, because they both stopped crying and agreed to let Craig drive. Craig and I shared a look of confused surprise, rolled our eyes, and shrugged it off as random good fortune that we had averted another crisis. We should have known better than to assume luck was on our side.

Since the girls had been born, it had become a family tradition that we go to Benihana for all of our birthday dinners. Benihana is a Japanese steakhouse in which the chef grills all of your food in front of you at your table. The tradition had been started for Gabe's sake. We had discovered

178

that Benihana was the one place we could take the girls and not have to deal with any meltdowns. The loud white noise of the exhaust fan was soothing. They loved to watch the chef's fancy tricks, not to mention that they devoured their entire platefuls of food. They clapped to the drum that accompanied the Happy Birthday song, and squealed with delight when ice cream was served at the end of every meal. So even though it was expensive to take a family of five there, it was worth every dime. We could actually celebrate Gabriel without the distraction of his temperamental twin sisters.

On the evening of Sydney and Taylor's third birthdays, there was a certain sense of liberation in the air. The girls had recently become potty-trained, so we traveled light since we were no longer slaves to the oversized diaper bag. At this point they accepted having to sit in high chairs, and no longer fought us on the matter. When we asked the girls what they wanted to eat, they could actually answer us: Pink pop and chicken. During our one trip to the bathroom, both girls willingly accepted my help in the stall. To top it off, the girls had requested to sit beside their big brother during dinner. So for the first time in three years, Craig and I actually got to sit next to each other. Instead of feeling like we were a traveling circus, we felt like a family. There was no tension coming from the kids, and Craig and I were getting along fabulously. Our collective mood was light and festive.

I had been waiting for this moment for three years. The revelation that my hard work, commitment and dedication were finally paying off was exhilarating. We were a happy family, after all! In order to celebrate, instead of my standard glass of wine I opted for a long island iced tea. Craig was amused by my bold order.

When the waitress delivered our drinks, the girls asked for a sip of mine since it looked like pop. I told them they couldn't have any because it was alcohol. They didn't object because they had been taught long ago that alcohol was only for grown-ups.

After the waitress left our table, I lifted my glass to Craig and proposed a toast.

"And just what are we toasting to?" he asked with playful anticipation.

As he raised his glass, I could tell he was enjoying my relaxed nature, too.

"To the girls not being *TWO anymore*!" I overdramatized.

We giggled as we clinked our glasses together. Then he leaned over and kissed me on the forehead, which he knows is my favorite place to be kissed by him. My heart swelled with love and gratitude. My husband was smiling at me, and my children were content beside me. I knew we had made it, and I couldn't have been any happier, prouder, or more relieved.

Two fun-filled hours later, we finished eating and paid the bill. We all held hands as we walked boisterously towards the exit of the restaurant. When we reached the lobby, I paused to fish for the keys in my purse. Naturally, per the girls' request, I had driven the family to the restaurant. When I found them, I handed them to Craig. I knew I'd had too much to drink to drive safely. While he didn't argue, he threw his head back to demonstrate the dread of impending twin objections when he took his place behind the wheel.

However, much to our surprise, Taylor put her fears to rest before we even exited the building. She had been paying more attention to us than we realized as we lingered in front of several dinner guests still waiting on their tables.

"No di, Momma! No di! You ha ow-o-hawl!" She ordered with great authority as she waved her little index finger in the air. Now she was laying down the law.

Craig and I grabbed all three of their hands as fast as we could and bolted through the exit door. We looked at each other with our eyes wide and our mouths agape in embarrassment. We couldn't hold back our laughter!

"Craig! Did you hear her???" I asked, hoping Taylor's words hadn't been as clear to him as they were to me.

"Yes, I heard her!" he responded in disbelief. "I think the whole restaurant heard her!"

"Do you think people understood what she said?" I asked fearfully.

"Ah, do you mean the part where your three-year-old told you not to drive because you had *alcohol?*" he sarcastically stated the obvious. "I don't know, but it's the clearest I've ever heard her talk!" He clutched his stomach in an effort to control his laughter.

"I know, *right?!*" I agreed emphatically. "Dear God! What have we *done??*" I asked him, scared of the unknown territory we had just entered.

"I'll tell you what we've done!" He was sure of his words. "We've paid thousands and thousands of dollars to get them to be able to say things like *that!*"

We could barely catch our breath. We laughed so hard we cried, and because it looked like fun, the kids laughed right along with us. Ya know what? Life was good again...because they weren't two anymore!

Chapter 23: Gaining Clarity

Our continued toughest uphill battle has been providing any means necessary to help the girls learn to talk clearly. Because we believed in our daughters and in our parental instincts, we never gave up on the girls' ability to conquer their disabilities. They have been labeled all sorts of things: sensory impaired, language impaired, Apraxic, and learning disabled just to name a few.

Every time we were given a label, we constructed a plan to defy that label. We were fortunate to live only twenty minutes away from Kaufman Children's Center, a world renowned practice for speech, language, sensory-motor and social connections. We learned and implemented Nancy Kaufman's speech language praxis materials at home in order to conquer the beasts of speech. The girls and I learned to identify the origin of sounds by using hand gestures to trigger correct pronunciations. For example, the /n/ sound was achieved by pointing to the bridge of our nose. The /k/ sound was made easier by making a chopping motion to our throat.

As long as we weren't in front of other people, I insisted they self-correct any mispronounced words that I knew they were capable of pronouncing correctly. I didn't allow them to be lazy with their speech because time was of the essence. On the few occasions they objected to my dedicated corrections, I reminded them how it felt to be the only kids in the class that weren't understood. By pre-school, they already felt isolated by their speech and were willing to make the effort to fix the problem.

Learning the letters of the alphabet proved to be very difficult for both girls. In order to make the task relative, I covered their alphabet flashcards with pictures of family members and friends that fit the appropriate letter. Gabe and Gi-Gi smiled for "G," Uncle Dusty, Da Da D. and Aunt Debra posed for "D," their babysitter Emmy was the face of "E," Grandpa Ted occupied T, their cousins Kendall, Lauren and Morgen took care of K, L, and M, etc. The girls were more willing to spend the extra time it took to learn their letters and beginning sounds because they enjoyed identifying the people they loved most.

Then, when I was told at their pre-school parent teacher conference that I had to face the fact that more than likely they would require special education services for learning impairments, I went to Target and bought Hooked on Phonics. It was a fact that Sydney and Taylor cooperated more readily with Craig than me. He had a soft spot for his little girls that afforded him great patience. He rarely raised his voice at them, and was happy to let me handle the vast majority of the discipline. The girls had even taken to calling him 'Daddy-Nice' when they addressed him. Craig enjoyed this term of endearment; he smiled from ear to ear, basking in the adoration from his daughters. I, of course, rolled my eyes dramatically with annoyed sarcasm. I will admit, though, that the loving bond Craig shared with the girls worked to our collective advantage. They looked forward to spending time with Daddy-Nice every night as they worked through the at-home reading program. Even in the moments the girls struggled with their lessons, Daddy-Nice knew just what to do to make it fun for them. Now, every time we listen to them read fluently and well-above grade level, I look at him and smile.

"Good job, babe." I tell him, and usually follow the endearing compliment with a hug or a kiss. "You did that," I give him credit.

"No, babe," he always says. "We did it." Even though I appreciate his admission of a joint effort, the real credit goes to Taylor and Sydney.

Just recently Taylor achieved full clarity and graduated from speech. Sydney still receives free services at school as she has yet to master her 'r' sound, but she at least falls within the normal range of other children her age. We have over six years and thousands of dollars invested into their speech and occupational therapy. So needless to say, we are very excited to see an end in sight.

Nevertheless, we still have some pronunciation work to do, as was evidenced by both of the girls recently. In anticipation of Gabriel's 10th birthday, Taylor informed me with great excitement that her brother would soon be a "double dipshit."

As I tried to relay Taylor's comedic reference to "double digit" to her great-grandmother, Sydney interrupted me.

"Momma?" she asked

"What, honey?" I answered.

"What does double dipshit mean?"

"You mean double digit," I corrected her.

"That's what I said," she told me. "Double dipshit."

But now instead of just being baffled by their joint mispronunciations, we can also afford to be amused. Time has taught us that, eventually, they will get it. As long as I don't have to translate their wedding vows, I will remain patient with the forward progress of their verbal abilities.

185

Despite all of this, both girls have managed to find a way to be secure and confident, even though at times they sound a little different than the rest of their classmates. And, believe it or not, their struggles with speech have proved to be a blessing in disguise. In enduring the humiliating scrutiny and judgment that goes along with being different, they have empathetic hearts and are very careful with the feelings of others. I am so proud of them for this.

They make friends easily, although their twin-bond is still stronger than any relationship I've ever known. In fact, I was determined to split them into separate classrooms to enable them to blossom independently of one another. However, after the first year of pre-school, it was obvious that they were much more comfortable with each other in the same environment than without. Sydney especially withdrew socially without the security blanket of her sister. She didn't speak to her teacher until April, and refused to speak in front of the class. As a result of her sudden drastic introversion, we placed them together for their second year of pre-school. When in the same learning environment, they began to thrive both socially and academically. And as they gained social confidence, they started to become more daring in their conversations with their classmates. In actuality, we found that when they were together in the same classroom there was radical improvement in their speech. Taylor was dismissed from private speech lessons from the Kaufman Children Center by the end of pre-school, and Sydney graduated in the middle of Kindergarten.

Together, our twin daughters have weathered every storm that has come their way. While it seemed at times the rain would never stop pouring, they continued to float light-heartedly. In the moments that I prayed for sunshine, they were busy searching for any and all rainbows.

Chapter 24: Figuring it out as we go...

All three of the kids have continued to keep us very busy, but the constant twin drama lessened drastically after the girls turned three. This is not to say that there weren't many bumps in the road along the way, which is obvious by the six years it has taken for me to finally complete this project.

Yes, it is true; we lost both of our daughters for a brief period of time on Halloween night the year they were four. We were Trick-or-Treating with a group of friends whose nine-year-old daughter was dressed as a dead bride. They were eager to follow her from house to house. However, on one ill-fated porch step they mistakenly followed a different dead bride in the opposite direction. Iron Man Gabriel had run too far ahead, and we were focused on reining him closer to us. When we looked back, Cinderella and Tinkerbell had disappeared. After suffering joint panic attacks, Craig and I finally located them across the street and five houses down. The girls never even knew they were missing. They were together, and they felt safe and secure. It didn't even occur to them to look for us.

The girls also continued to defy us more than Gabriel ever did, but most often it was when one was daring the other to do something. For example, there was a period of time when I couldn't get them to leave their five-point harnesses fastened in their car seats. They would race to unbuckle to see who could do it the fastest. Even though I screamed at them from the front seat about their lack of safety, they were not fazed. No matter what I did, I couldn't get them to take this matter seriously.

Then one day we were taking a walk in our sub-division. Since there are no sidewalks, we were walking on the right side of the road when we came upon a garter snake that had been run over by a car.

"Ewww...Momma!" one of them exclaimed. "What's *that?*"

"Yuck," I agreed. "That's a dead snake."

"What happened to it, Momma?" they wanted to know.

"Well, that snake didn't listen to its mommy," I seized the moment.

"What do you mean, Momma?" one of them asked. Their curiosity was peaked.

"Well, girls," I explained very seriously, "that snake's mommy said to hold her hand when he was crossing the street, but he didn't listen. Because he didn't listen to his mommy when she was trying to keep him safe, he got hit by a car and died."

"Oh, no!" one of them said with her eyes wide. "Was the mommy sad?"

"Oh yes, girls! The mommy was *very* sad!" I assured them both. "Because if her little snake would have listened to her when she was trying to keep him safe, he would still be alive to hug and kiss her. Instead, her snake is dead and she doesn't have anyone to hug and kiss anymore." While this seemed to be an extreme fabrication of the truth, desperate times with twins called for desperate measures.

"That's sad, Momma," one of them sympathized.

"I know it's sad, girls. So you need to start listening to me when I try to keep you safe so that this doesn't happen to one of you, okay?" I pleaded.

"Okay, Momma," they both agreed.

When Craig returned home from work that day, I told him about our run-in with the dead snake. I felt as though I had made a connection with them, even if it was a bit of a stretch. He was skeptical. However, that very evening we went out to dinner as a family. On our way home, the girls decided to play their "unbuckle" game. After telling them to buckle back up twice to no avail, Craig uncharacteristically lost his temper.

He pulled over into an empty parking lot and brought the car to an immediate stop, intentionally throwing the girls forward in their seats hard enough to scare them. Both stunned, they looked up at their father who was obviously furious. Daddy-Nice had reached his limit. He was tired of them risking their safety in the car, so he turned around and yelled at his daughters right from the driver's seat.

"*Girls!*" he shouted to be sure he had their full attention. "Do you want to get dead like the snake???"

"No, Daddy-Nice, No!" They burst into tears. "NO!!!"

"Well, okay, then!" he concluded. "Buckle your seatbelts and listen to your mommy and daddy! Or else you will get dead like the snake!"

The girls' little hands buckled their belts as fast as they possibly could. This was the last time they *ever* unbuckled in the car. In fact, to this very day, if we pull away before they are completely buckled, they both experience a high level of anxiety.

"Wait!" the unbuckled girl will holler in panic. "I'm not buckled, and I don't want to get dead like the snake!"

We chuckle every time, but we earned the right. Teaching them discipline was accomplished one small victory at a time; every time we took a step forward, there always seemed to be a few twin steps back.

Even as they got older, Gabe continued to get the short end of the stick while we were trying to keep up with his little sisters - like the time we accidentally left him in the car on a freezing wintery night.

The girls were five and Gabe was seven on this auspicious occasion. We were visiting my dad to celebrate Christmas, and had decided to switch things up and go out for a Mexican Fiesta in lieu of our traditional sit-down family dinner. The roads were covered with snow and ice from the winter storm that had hit a few hours earlier. The parking lot at the restaurant hadn't yet been plowed or salted, and I was concerned the kids would slip and hurt themselves as they hopped out of the car. In order to prevent this from occurring, I grabbed a hand of each of the girls and assisted them out of the van. I continued to hold on to them tightly as we walked across the sheet of black ice to the restaurant entrance. Since I had stopped to help both girls, I assumed Craig would take care of Gabriel's safe exit from the other side of the van.

After we checked in and were shown to our long table in the back of the restaurant, I started to strategically seat all the kids. I helped to make sure the youngest cousins were near adult help. Then I worked to group the girls together, and then the boys. On two different occasions, I stopped someone from sitting in the seat that I was saving for Gabe.

"Don't sit there," I instructed on both instances. "Gabe is going to want to sit by Ryan."

I looked up to find my son who wasn't taking his seat at the dinner table. "Where *is* Gabe?" I asked puzzled.

Just then, my seven-year-old little boy burst into our private room in a state of emotional hysteria. Sobbing uncontrollably, his face was drenched with tears.

"Gabriel! What's wrong??" I had no idea what was bothering him. I squatted down to hug him.

"Mommy!" he yelled through sobs. "You left me in the car!"

I could tell by his tone that his feelings were more than hurt; they were broken.

"What do you mean I left you in the car?" I asked, completely baffled.

"You helped the girls get out, and then you shut the door before I could get out!" his tone was full of hate.

"Buddy! I'm so sorry!" I apologized, feeling like a terrible mother. "But why didn't you just open the door and follow me?" I asked, trying to make sense of the situation.

"*Because!*" he screamed as snot bubbled out of his nose. "You locked the door!" He was furious with me now.

"Gabriel, I didn't even have the keys, honey!" I tried to comfort him, but it wasn't working.

"I couldn't get out! I was pounding and pounding on the window, but nobody could hear me!" he continued to scold me, as though I meant for him to be left alone in the freezing car.

"How did you get out, sweetie?" I asked. My heart sank further with every question.

"I went to the driver's door and it opened up," he explained. "And then I had to run across the parking lot in the dark all by myself!"

"Oh, sweetie! I am so *sorry!*" I held him close until he could get himself settled. I felt awful. Neglectful guilt nearly knocked me over. "It was an accident, Gabe. I never would have shut the door on you had I known you were coming my way. I thought you were with Daddy!" I tried to defend myself honestly.

"Well, I *wasn't*" he emphasized the obvious.

I looked at Craig, who was suspiciously quiet while witnessing his son's explanation of sheer terror.

"Craig, what were you doing while you were walking into the restaurant?" I demanded.

"Ah...I was talking to your dad," he answered sheepishly.

"Right," I agreed bitterly. "And how many kids did I have?" I threw the question at him.

"I'm assuming two?" I couldn't believe he had the nerve to ask.

"That's right," I glared at him. "And how many did you have?"

"Ah...zero?" he answered quietly as he shoved his hands in his pockets and avoided eye contact.

"Right. Do you see a problem there?" I berated him.

"I didn't mean to, babe!" he tried to defend himself.

"Well, why don't you explain that to your son?" I suggested as I walked away and left him to deal with his son's hatred for both of us. While Gabe eventually forgave us, he still harbors a fear that we will leave him somewhere. It's never happened again, but I can't say that I blame him.

Craig and I can admit with ease that none of our parenting has been perfect, but somehow we have managed to persevere; even when the wheels felt like they would never stop turning. Raising our children has

193

taken an unbelievable amount of patience, flexibility, communication, humility, and teamwork. As a result, we are bigger, better and stronger as a couple. Had someone told me this was going to be the outcome when the twins first happened, I would have been skeptical. But, so far, we've navigated through the rough parts to build a home full of love and stability.

However, I fear it just might be necessary to write another book when they all hit puberty... Just saying.

Chapter 25: Reflection

Now that I understand and accept the girls' zest for life, more often than not they leave me inspired instead of frustrated. Everything they do together is an artistic adventure. Whether it's having impromptu tea parties in their bathroom, or intricately planning and constructing Fairy Houses during the summer, or even ice-skating in a box of powdered Tide, they have fun doing it. Isn't that what life is all about? It certainly is when your best friend is your identical twin.

While staying at home with the kids was more challenging than I could have ever imagined, I'm glad I weathered the storm. My chaotic experiences as a stay-at-home-mother caused me to grow as a person. I now approach life with a sense of humor, and I no longer sweat the small stuff. I refrain from passing judgement on others, because I learned the only way to really know what something feels like is to live it. I love to spend quiet time alone now, as that was a luxury I could not afford just a few years ago. Through the curveballs of cancer, the NICU, and the constant unexpected nature of the twins I learned to adapt quicker to whatever challenges life presents us. I accept that we are not invincible, nor will life ever go according to plan. I no longer try to control my destiny, just my reactions to it.

I share intense bonds with each of my children that I believe were cultivated during our collective survival of the early years of their childhood. They learned there was nothing they could do that I wouldn't love them through. They trust me to keep them safe, and look to me for guidance when they're unsure of themselves. It is easy for me to let them move on to each phase of their life because I never feel as though I need to make up for lost time. Every day offers a new adventure, and I look forward to them all. Because who knows what crazy story I'll have to tell next?

*photo credit Nicole Barczak
http://www.nbarczak.com/

43180984R00111

Made in the USA
Lexington, KY
21 July 2015